Fundamentals of educational planning—31

Included in the series:*

1. *What is Educational Planning?*
   Philip H. Coombs
2. *The Relation of Educational Plans to Economic and Social Planning*
   R. Poignant
3. *Educational Planning and Human Resource Development*
   F. Harbison
4. *Planning and the Educational Administrator*
   C. E. Beeby
5. *The Social Context of Educational Planning*
   C. A. Anderson
6. *The Costing of Educational Plans*
   J. Vaizey, J. D. Chesswas
7. *The Problems of Rural Education*
   V. L. Griffiths
8. *Educational Planning: The Adviser's Role*
   Adam Curle
9. *Demographic Aspects of Educational Planning*
   Ta Ngoc Châu
10. *The Analysis of Educational Costs and Expenditure*
    J. Hallak
11. *The Professional Identity of the Educational Planner*
    Adam Curle
12. *The Conditions for Success in Educational Planning*
    G. C. Ruscoe
13. *Cost-benefit Analysis in Educational Planning*
    Maureen Woodhall
14. *Educational Planning and Unemployed Youth*
    Archibald Callaway
15. *The Politics of Educational Planning in Developing Countries*
    C. D. Rowley
16. *Planning Education for a Plural Society*
    Chai Hon-Chan
17. *Planning the Primary School Curriculum in Developing Countries*
    H. W. R. Hawes
18. *Planning Educational Assistance for the Second Development Decade*
    H. M. Phillips
19. *Study Abroad and Educational Development*
    William D. Carter
20. *Realistic Educational Planning*
    K. R. McKinnon
21. *Planning Education in Relation to Rural Development*
    G. M. Coverdale
22. *Alternatives and Decisions in Educational Planning*
    John D. Montgomery
23. *Planning the School Curriculum*
    Arieh Lewy
24. *Cost Factors in Planning Educational Technological Systems*
    Dean T. Jamison
25. *The Planner and Lifelong Education*
    Pierre Furter
26. *Education and Employment: a Critical Appraisal*
    Martin Carnoy
27. *Planning Teacher Demand and Supply*
    Peter Williams
28. *Planning Early Childhood Care and Education in Developing Countries*
    Alastair Heron
29. *Communication Media in Education for Low-Income Countries*
    Emile G. McAnany and John K. Mayo
30. *The Planning of Nonformal Education*
    David R. Evans

* Also published in French. Other titles to appear

Education, training and the traditional sector

Jacques Hallak and Françoise Caillods

Paris 1981
Unesco: International Institute for Educational Planning

The Swedish International Development Authority (SIDA)
has provided financial assistance for the publication of this booklet

Published in 1981 by the United Nations
Educational, Scientific and Cultural Organization
7 Place de Fontenoy, 75700 Paris
Printed by Ceuterick, Louvain

Cover design by Bruno Pfäffli
ISBN 92-803-1097-6

© Unesco 1981
Printed in Belgium

Fundamentals of educational planning

The booklets in this series are written primarily for two types of clientele: those engaged in—or preparing for—educational planning and administration, especially in developing countries; and others, less specialized, such as senior government officials and policy-makers who seek a more general understanding of educational planning and of how it is related to overall national development. They are devised to be of use either for private study or in formal training programmes.

Since this series was launched in 1967 the practice as well as the concept of educational planning has undergone substantial change. Many of the assumptions which underlay earlier attempts to put some rationality into the process of educational development have been abandoned or at the very least criticized. At the same time, the scope of educational planning itself has been broadened. In addition to the formal system of schools, it now includes other important educational efforts in non-formal settings and among adults. Attention to the growth and expansion of educational systems is being supplemented and sometimes even replaced by a growing concern for the distribution of educational opportunities and benefits across different regions and across social, ethnic and sex groups. The planning, implementation and evaluation of innovations and reforms in the content and substance of education is becoming at least as important a preoccupation of educational planners and administrators as the forecasting of the size of the educational system and its output. Moreover, the planning process itself is changing, giving more attention to the implementation and evaluation of plans as well as to their design, and exploring such possibilities as integrated planning, participatory planning, and micro-planning.

One of the purposes of these booklets is to reflect this diversity by giving different authors, coming from a wide range of backgrounds and disciplines, the opportunity to express their ideas and to communicate their experience on various aspects of changing theories and practices in educational planning.

Although the series has been carefully planned, no attempt has been made to avoid differences or even contradictions in the views expressed by the authors. The Institute itself does not wish to impose any official doctrine on any planner. Thus, while the views are the responsibility of the authors and may not always be shared by Unesco or the IIEP, they are believed to warrant attention in the international forum of ideas.

Since readers will vary so widely in their backgrounds, the authors have been given the difficult task of introducing their subjects from the beginning, explaining technical terms that may be commonplace to some but a mystery to others, and yet adhering to scholarly standards. This approach will have the advantage, it is hoped, of making the booklets optimally useful to every reader.

Preface

The existence of segmentation in the modes of production of goods and services has long been recognized by planners and economists in developing countries. The modern sector, highly productive, capital-intensive and offering high salaries—as opposed to the traditional sector, covering all sorts of non-wage activities—was considered until recently as the principal dynamic source of development. Thus the main labour problem to be tackled was the lack of qualified manpower and the low qualification level of the labour force. It was assumed that, as industrialization takes place, employment in the modern sector would expand and gradually take over that in the traditional sector. It is now increasingly realised that this analysis has not been borne out in reality. Over the last ten years, most developing countries have witnessed both an acceleration of rural exodus and a slow rate of job creation in the modern sector; this has resulted in high rates of un- and under-employment in urban areas. The education systems have produced more school-leavers, diploma-holders and graduates than the labour markets have been able to absorb, and unemployment of school-leavers is now a matter of growing concern in most countries. One cannot be satisfied with the fact that unemployment has not increased as fast as was predicted from the mismatch between job creation and new arrivals on the labour market. Another apparent paradox is that rural-urban migrations continue to increase, in spite of the apparent lack of employment opportunities in the cities. This could not be explained if the development of various activities which can be grouped under what is known as the "traditional sector"—such as, for instance: handicrafts, small trades, small services, transport and construction—had not taken place to satisfy the needs of the poorer segment of the population, tourists, etc.

Recently, together with a shift of emphasis in development priorities, the traditional sector has been given increasing attention, as a sector which would potentially increase job opportuni-

Preface

ties, generate income and help fight poverty in urban areas. Various educational policies and reforms have been designed to facilitate access to the traditional sector and encourage self-employment of school-leavers.

These are the reasons why the IIEP has undertaken a review of the existing literature on the relationship between education, training and employment in the traditional sector. The authors are Jacques Hallak and Françoise Caillods, IIEP staff members. They start with a discussion of the various theories concerned with the origin, rôle and evolution of the traditional sector in a developing economy. They emphasize that there is no dichotomy between the modern and traditional sectors, but rather a continuum of situations starting from marginal and residual jobs on the one hand, up to direct-wage employment in big administrations and enterprises on the other, and propose a typology in five sub-sectors, each with its own characteristics and evolution prospects.

Analysing the results of existing studies in Africa, Latin America and Asia, they draw the profile of the "standard worker" in the traditional sector, which gives us some insight into the criteria for access to that sector. They then examine the rôle of formal education and informal apprenticeship in the development of the traditional sector, and their impact on its productivity. Apprenticeship, in many developing countries, plays the dual rôle of imparting the necessary skills to workers on the one hand, and providing cheap manpower on the other, thus allowing the reproduction of this subsistence sector; this is a clear example of the very complex relationship existing between education and employment, and shows the necessity to place this discussion in the overall context of the political economy of development. From this analysis the authors draw a number of conclusions for educational planning, both in the short and long run, which are likely to stimulate discussion. We hope that these conclusions will interest educational planners and policy-makers in developing countries—to whom this book is primarily addressed—but as a "state of the art" study, based on many documents of limited circulation and difficult access, this booklet should also interest many researchers.

Michel Debeauvais
Director, IIEP

Contents

Introduction 11

I. Elements of the methodological debate 17

II. Profiles of workers in the traditional sector 37

III. Education, training and access to the traditional sector . . 82

IV. The contribution of education/training to production in the traditional sector 107

Appendixes 128

Bibliography 138

Introduction

It has become a commonplace to observe that economic growth guarantees neither higher employment levels nor fairer income distribution.

Figures for Latin America show that Gross Domestic Product has risen at an annual average of 2 per cent since 1945; during the same period, the number of families living below the poverty line has either increased or, in the most favourable cases, remained stable (*1*).[1]

In spite of the problems involved in extracting general trends valid for Africa, Latin America and Asia (with which continents this paper is concerned), we can describe problems of employment by contrasting a certain number of trends:

1. Population growth in the 1950s and 60s is responsible for the expansion of the present population of working age, whose growth rate has risen from 2-2.5 per cent p.a. to 2.5-3 per cent p.a. These average rates conceal differences between town and country (urban population growth is four times greater, on average, than that of rural populations).
2. The imprecision of available data nothwithstanding, it can be stated that under-employment in agriculture fluctuates around 35 per cent (is at any rate superior to 25 per cent), and that industrial employment is growing slowly, much less rapidly than industrial output (in the Philippines, for example, value added in manufacturing industry grew at annual rate of 8.8 per cent and 8.6 per cent in the periods 1956-62 and 1962-68,

---

1. Numbers in brackets refer to the Bibliography (pp. 138-143).

while the corresponding figures for employment were 5.2 per cent and 6 per cent).
3. High urban population growth rates, stimulated by migration, far outrun the creation of new jobs. This often produces very high unemployment rates in the cities: 12.7 per cent in Jakarta (2); 12 per cent in Asunción; 20 per cent (31 per cent in the slums) in Managua (1); 15.2 per cent in Nairobi (4). This unemployment mainly hits the least socially vulnerable categories from the point of view of income (young people and women who are not heads of households).[1] Certain estimates give the unemployment rate for the 25-54 age-group as between one-quarter and one-half the rate for young people and women.[2]
4. In spite of this unemployment, differences in pay and living standards between town and country have attracted migrants to the towns. The wages of barely skilled labour in the towns appear to be significantly higher than in the country (even if we take into account unemployment and under-employment)(3). This suggests that rural labour is under-employed to a greater extent than urban labour.

1. In the Philippines in 1972 the unemployment rate was estimated at 2.1 per cent for heads of households and at 9.3 per cent for other categories. It was 3.6 per cent for the over-24s, and 12.4 per cent for the 15-24 age-group. In Kenya in 1969-70 the unemployment rate among adult heads of households stood at 4.2 per cent in Nairobi, 9.8 per cent in Mombasa, and 4 per cent in Kisumu; the corresponding figures for unmarried women were 50 per cent in Nairobi, 67.2 per cent in Mombasa, and 50.4 per cent in Kisumu.
2. In Kenya in 1968-69 the percentages of heads of households and of other adult members of household unemployed or (in the case of women) whose work is confined to domestic tasks were as follows:

City	Heads of Household	Other adult members		
		Male	Female Married	Female Unmarried
Nairobi	4.2	15.2	77.5	50.0
Mombasa	9.8	20.0	85.1	67.2
Kisumu	4.0	11.7	86.1	50.4

SOURCE Republic of Kenya, *Urban household budget survey, 1968-69* (unpublished).

TABLE 1. Urban and rural unemployment rates (percentage of working population)

Country	Year	Urban unemployment	Rural unemployment
Africa			
Algeria	1966	26.6	—
Burundi	1963	18.7	—
Cameroon	1964	4.6	3.4
Cameroon	1966	15.0	—
Ghana	1960	11.6	—
Ivory Coast	1963	20.0	—
Morocco	1960	20.5	5.4
Nigeria	1963	12.6	—
Tanzania	1965	7.0	3.9
Zaïre	1967	12.9	—
America			
Argentina	1968	5.4	—
Bolivia	1966	13.2	—
Chile	1968	6.1	2.0
Colombia	1967	15.5	—
Costa Rica	1966-67	5.6	—
El Salvador	1961	6.6	—
Guatemala	1964	5.4	—
Guyana	1965	20.5	—
Honduras	1961	7.8	—
Jamaica	1960	19.0	12.4
Dutch Antilles	1966	16.0	—
Panama	1960	15.5	3.6
Panama	1967	9.3	2.8
Peru	1964	4.2	—
Peru	1969	5.2	—
Uruguay	1963	10.9	2.3
Venezuela	1961	17.5	4.3
Venezuela	1964	16.4	—
Venezuela	1968	6.5	3.1
Asia			
India	1961-62	3.2	1.7
Indonesia	1961	8.5	—
Iran	1956	4.5	1.8
Iran	1966	5.5	11.3
Korea	1963-64	7.0	1.8
Malaysia (Western)	1967	11.6	7.4
Philippines	1967	13.1	6.9
Singapore	1966	9.1	—
Sri Lanka	1959-60	14.3	10.0
Syrian Arab Republic	1967	7.3	—
Thailand	1966	2.8	—

SOURCE ILO. Urban employment in developing countries.

In all, the economic growth observed in certain countries in the course of the last quarter-century has been matched not by a fall in unemployment rates, but by a fall in under-employment in both town and country, and by the development of a sector of the economy that absorbs surplus labour arising from migration to the towns. The new jobs created in the towns are filled either by under-employed country or townspeople or by ex-urban unemployed, who thereby deprive newcomers to the towns of job opportunities.

In this respect, the economic growth actually experienced in different countries has been essentially heterogeneous, in the sense that the modernization being brought about by business has spread irregularly throughout the different areas of the economy. These may be classified into two sectors.

Firstly, a small modern sector, highly capital-intensive, with high productivity, high wages, highly structured in terms of working conditions, and with a limited absorption capacity in terms of manpower.

Secondly, a traditional sector, with low productivity, very low wages, pretty well unorganized, encompassing a very broad spectrum of activities from the shoeshine boy, construction labourer, street pedlar and artisan to the head of a small workshop employing a handful of workers. This sector seems to have developed a great deal through the expansion of existing activities and through the emergence of new activities generated by the need of the working population (migrant or otherwise) to find some means of subsistence.

This traditional sector, which may occupy up to 60 per cent of the work force in the towns (see, for example, Table 2) has come to embody, in recent years, all the hopes of coping with the problem of unemployment,[1] especially since about ten years ago a delegation from the ILO World Employment Programme in Kenya, noting the importance of the informal sector in cities such as Nairobi and Mombasa, concluded that:

> "The informal sector offers a great many people an opportunity of earning a livelihood. Although it is often regarded as unproductive

1. According to Bairoch, the salaried employment index has increased slightly since 1950, with a few exceptions however (Abidjan, Brazzaville, Pointe Noire, Nouakchott and Libreville); as a percentage of the population of working age, there has been a general fall in salaried employment.

TABLE 2. The informal (traditional) sector as a percentage of the urban workforce in different countries

Country and city	Income criterion	Occupational criterion
Brazil (1972)		
States of Rio de Janeiro and Sao Paolo	24	—
Chile (1968)		
Urban total	—	39
Dominican Republic (1973)		
Santo Domingo	50	—
Ecuador (1970)		
Guayaquil	48	—
Quito	48	—
El Salvador (1974)		
San Salvador	41	46
Mexico (1970)		
Federal District and State of Mexico	27	—
Paraguay (1973)		
Asunción	—	57
Peru (1970)		
Urban total	—	60
Venezuela (1974)		
Urban total	—	44
Caracas	—	40

SOURCE PREALC, based on official figures. The Mexican figures are drawn from population census returns. The figures for the other countries are based on household surveys. For Peru, see R. Webb (1974), and for Venezuela, see H. Pereira and M. Zink (1976).

and stagnant, in our view it offers a vast spectrum of goods and services at low cost, making intensive and competitive use of labour..." (*4*).

From the point of view of educational planning (which is what this volume is concerned with), i.e., the relations between education, training and the traditional or informal sector, two key questions arise: firstly, what is the role of education/training in generating and developing the traditional sector? and secondly, can education/training contribute effectively to reducing unemployment by improving the performance of the traditional sector? Even though the abundant recent literature on the traditional sector has generally treated these questions as purely incidental, it does nevertheless contain material that could prove useful in formulating answers, which will be presented in three of the chapters of this report: standard profiles of workers in the traditional sector (Chapter II); the role of education/training—and of apprenticeship, especially—in the development of the traditional sector (Chapter III); the contribution of education/training to production in the traditional sector (Chapter IV). As a prelude, Chapter I will seek to establish the conceptual framework of our analysis, by briefly contrasting the different theoretical views concerning the origins and outlook of the traditional sector in the economic evolution of the developing countries.[1] In spite of the existence of a large traditional sector in rural areas, and the complexity of the relationship linking the rural sector and the rural traditional sector to the urban traditional sector and the urban modern sector, we have limited ourselves to analysing the traditional sector in urban areas.

---

1. We refer here to the countries of Africa, Asia (excluding Japan), and Latin America (including Mexico and Central America).

I. Elements of the methodological debate

In the Introduction we have implicitly defined the "traditional", "non-formal" or "unstructured" sector [1] as the residual sector in the towns, which absorbs surplus labour that is employed in neither the modern nor the intermediate sectors. The difficulty surrounding discussion of this theme is twofold: to begin with, how are we to postulate as an object of study a sector that is by nature heterogeneous? secondly, assuming that it was possible to circumscribe the sector, labour is free to enter it and leave it over the course of time, which considerably complicates the business of analysing the nature of training and education needs in this sector.

A. Activities in the traditional sector

By way of example, Appendix I contains a typology (list of activities) of the traditional sector drawn from the work of the IEDES research team (7). The way activities belonging to this sector are grouped together, or the criteria used in delimiting them (see in particular the ILO report on Kenya), implicitly postulate theoretical assumptions about the origins and position of this sector in the economic history of the countries concerned.

---

1. For the sake of convenience, in what follows we shall refer solely to the "traditional" sector, none of the terms suggested by the different authors being wholly satisfactory.

1. Classical dualist models

These models are based on a highly empirical observation of the actual situation, dividing it into two sectors (modern and traditional), each governed by specific rules. "In place of the former modern/traditional sector dichotomy, we now find an opposition between the formal and the informal sector (Hart), structured and unstructured (Weeks, Sethuranam), modern and transitional sectors (Bugnicourt, Penouil), upper and lower circuits (Santos), corporate and bazaar economies (Geertz)" (5). All these distinctions are based on empirical criteria employed to circumscribe the traditional sector, namely: the difficulty of statistical observation; ease of access to activities; family-owned businesses; labour-intensive methods; unregulated markets wide open to competition; incomes sometimes illicit or undeclared; occasional or temporary activities; labour market unprotected, no social insurance, etc.

Rapid growth in the former, highly capital-intensive, sector was expected to absorb labour from the latter. For observers of the situation in the developing countries, in the 1950s and 1960s, the main question concerning employment was that of a shortage of qualified labour and its unsuitability for modern industry. Ten years later, with the completion of decolonization (in Africa) and/or acceptance of the aims of the First United Nations Development Decade, most countries had been radically transformed, especially in terms of demography, education and the economy. The employment issue had shifted, becoming: how are we to cope with excess labour supply and disguised or open unemployment in the towns? The solutions proposed were: firstly, to adopt a development strategy centred on specialization in highly labour-intensive activities; secondly, by taking measures to develop the modern sector at the expense of the traditional sector, with its very low productivity, looked on as a factor of under-employment or disguised unemployment.

Now that the facts have shown this empirical model to be wrong, recent modifications to it have taken two directions:
1. Noting the great heterogeneity of the traditional sector, are we to treat licit and illicit (prostitution, smuggling, etc.), regular (artisans) and irregular (street pedlars) activities alike? Certain authors have subdivided the traditional sector into two subsectors (11), holding that one was doomed to stagnation and subsequently to extinction (low productivity, unsuitable tech-

nology, heavy competition, etc.), while the other, more "modern" and potentially promising, would be capable of generating income with a multiplier effect on employment. This led to the proposal to protect and encourage small production units by means of specific measures, that the modern sector should sub-contract work out to the most promising traditional sub-sector.

2. Other specialists pointed out that, given that unemployment was persisting and growing worse—the facts are stubborn—the classical dualist scenario was up against a brick wall. Consequently they prefer to stand the scenario on its head. As we pointed out in the introduction, the last ten years have witnessed both a quickening of the rural exodus and a poor rate of job creation in the modern sector; the exodus can be accounted for by wage and income differentials between town and country; but in order to account for the low rate of job creation several factors need to be taken into consideration: (i) the modern sector tends to employ highly capital-intensive production methods with very low capital/labour ratios; (ii) as between the modern and the traditional sectors, "intermediate" activities, defined as those having medium capital/labour coefficients, none the less necessitate enough fixed capital for this to constitute an obstacle to entrance (9); (iii) lastly, the growing inequalities of income observed in most countries are a limiting factor on solvent demand and, consequently, on the growth of the modern and intermediate sectors. As a result, the problem of employment cannot be dissociated from that of income; these countries' economic problem is not one of growth alone, but also of equity (since growth has proved slow in a context of mounting inequality). It is therefore necessary to boost demand and satisfy basic needs. It was at that time that *Redistribution with growth* (*10*), a joint work, was published under the auspices of the World Bank. The growth strategies proposed in this book coupled the fight against unemployment with the fight against poverty; it recommended the simultaneous evening-out of the distribution of incomes, the satisfying of people's basic needs, and the halting of the pauperization of the peasantry in order to cut back the rural exodus. To protect small production units in the traditional sector from the competition of the modern sector it suggested,

for example, that modern industries be organized and encouraged to sub-contract work out to small units in the traditional sector, offering the latter contracts on reasonable, guaranteed, terms. Theoretical models were devised to show that all these objectives could be pursued simultaneously, and that all that was wanted was to apply the requisite policies.

Unfortunately, experience has shown that dualist analyses were over-optimistic in their assessment of the likely evolution of the balance of power in developing economies: efforts to combat inequality always trigger defensive reactions on the part of dominant groups and normally entail coercive action, not always in harmony with the aims of the political régimes in question (12). Further, surveys conducted in recent years have revealed the fragility of dualist models, particularly in their neglect of the historical dimensions of the development problem. What is more, certain authors state that they lose their illusions as they observe:

1. That solvent demand for the goods and services of the traditional sector remains sluggish, at all events inferior to supply; consequently, despite measures to encourage the traditional sector, the development of its activities has failed to flourish and unemployment persists.
2. That on the pretext of protecting small production units in order to foster their transition to the modern sector, public subsidies generally end up in the pockets of agents outside the artisan sector (13), avid for quick additional gains, competing with the small-scale producers on their own ground (recruitment of apprentices, confiscation of markets); in tropical Africa, for instance, certain civil servants have seized on the advantages to be had from the state's concern for small-scale production and invested, either directly or indirectly, in the traditional sector, opening workshops (clothing, joinery, mechanical repairs) run by "apprentice-businessmen" who often happen to be relatives. The school supplies' market, for example (desks, chairs, etc.) has provided certain businessmen/officials with an opportunity of boosting their incomes significantly.
3. That, on the other hand, certain activities have graduated from the artisan stage to the modern sector (bakeries in Abidjan, for example), but to the detriment of the object of creating jobs.

4. That in any case, the policy being pursued by certain countries aimed at structuring the activities of the traditional sector, boosting earnings distributed in this sector, organizing access to it, etc., has naturally led to the marginalization of almost all activities, with the exception of a few small units made profitable through state support.

The underlying weakness of dualist analyses—even in their more elaborate forms which divide the traditional sector into two sub-sectors—stems from the fact that they simply assimilate several essentially heterogeneous activities to one or two objects of study and action; from their neglect of interactions between different activities, and particularly their implicit assumption that the residual traditional sector (smuggling, prostitution, street peddling) will gradually disappear; and finally, from their lack of historical perspective on the origins and evolution of activities belonging to the traditional sector.

2. Radical analyses

Alongside the development of dualist models, and more recently in an effort to take account of their shortcomings, other aproaches have emerged. Their sources of inspiration have been diverse, but they do have in common (i) the importance they place on the role of capital and its accumulation in the interpretation of the traditional sector, (ii) their emphasis on the connections that exist between different activities in the modern and traditional sectors, rejecting any form of reductionist analysis entailing the independent application of economic concepts (consumption, output, employment, income, etc.) to individual sub-sectors. It was therefore tempting to label these approaches (Marxist or) neo-Marxist; even though these authors are far from unanimous, it is worth supplying a few pointers to help assess their contribution to the methodological discussion:

(a) *Capital and its accumulation.* The coexistence, at a given moment in time, of large modern international-scale industries with the most archaic forms of production of goods and services may be accounted for by the historical process of the development of capitalism, which may very broadly be presented thus:
— production for domestic consumption. Raw materials are processed at home to satisfy the family's needs. Even in industrial

countries such as France, for example, some families still make their own cheese, ham or wines. In Marxist terms, these have no value in exchange, only value in use;
— production to order. This involves one-off items made to order by artisans who earn their living from occasional work, outside the normal trade circuits;
— small-scale commodity production (sometimes called cottage industry). Here, goods and services are offered for sale independent of any specific order. This means tying up raw materials and tools, hence a little capital. This leads to the emergence of values in use and values in exchange;
— small capitalist enterprises. With the expansion of the market, certain types of commodity production become transformed and undergo a change of nature: they need capital to develop. Since capital is in the hands of the merchants, these small businesses come under the control of commercial capital (this can happen in numerous different ways), which in turn becomes transformed into industrial capital. The number of employees grows, at the expense of handicrafts; labour force becomes a commodity and the conditions now exist for the development of capitalism.

In a word, according to this scenario the traditional sector, which serves as an indicator of economic evolution, is supposed to disappear gradually under pressure of competition from the modern sector, unless its preservation should turn out to favour the development of capitalism, or unless it manages to survive marginally.

(b) *Extracting surplus value.* A number of authors (jointly described by the PREALC as theoreticians of "subordination" (*1*) in a recent publication) have developed Marx's writings on surplus value and now assert that the survival of the traditional sector is necessary to the accumulation of capital and raising of the rate of profit. Putting things in a resolutely worldwide perspective, they attribute the birth of capitalism and the process of accumulation to the extraction of surplus value. In this light, small-scale activities (the traditional sector) appear either as the emergence of a national capitalism on a reduced (peripheral) scale, following in the wake of large-scale capitalism (central), or/and as the small producers' response to the development of peripheral capitalism, or/

and as a means of survival for small-scale producers on the road to proletarianization and pauperization (5). In any case, a transfer of values from the traditional sector to the modern sector occurs (i) through uneven exchange—exchange of products in whose manufacture the disparity of wages is superior to the difference in productivity (14), (ii) through the non-existent or low return on capital in the traditional sector and the high rates of profit in the modern sector; (iii) and/or through a return on capital proportionate to the capital intensity of the sectors under consideration.

(c) *The constituent parts of the traditional sector and their evolution.* This naturally leads us to identify two groups of activity within the traditional sector depending on their relations with capitalism, namely the commodity and the non-commodity production sectors. This distinction is crucial if we are to hazard any forecast whatever as to the future of the traditional sector (it is an outgrowth of the notions of exchange value and use value):
— the non-commodity production sub-sector comprises services and work that create value in use, which are remunerated, and which may be regarded as unproductive (e.g. domestic servants, shoeshine boys). This sub-sector in a manner of speaking lies "outside" the modern capitalist sector; its outlook is dubious on the assumption of growth based on increasing capital-intensity of production;
— the petty commodity production sub-sector (or cottage industry) refers to activities that create value in exchange, and hence goods for sale to end or intermediate (sub-contracting) users. This sector maintains contradictory (dialectical) links with the modern sector; it may exist as a parasite, be plundered, serve as an appendix to capitalism, be exploited, or even be simply independent of the modern sector. Depending on the activities it comprises, the commodity production sub-sector may thus appear to be a remnant doomed to extinction, a contribution to the accumulation of capital, or as being justified independently of any direct link with capital through its place in a strategy of a-capitalist development.

The reproduction of dependent (or subordinate) activities is assured by a low-paid proletariat and the non-depreciation of fixed capital, hence *despite* confiscation of the surplus. In independent activities, production is aimed at partitioned markets, for specific social strata, but the question as to the transfer of values between these activities and the modern sector remains unanswered: who pays the customers for these activities, and how? As A. Morice puts it, "when an apprentice works for no wage at all for an artisan who could not survive otherwise, to manufacture a product (a pair of shoes for example) for sale to an employee from the modern sector (thereby providing the said employee's employer with low-cost reproduction of labour power), who is exploiting whom?" (*15*).

In all, completeness imperatively requires of these radical analyses separate treatment of the specific problem of the reproduction of labour power, and of the general problem of relations between the different categories of labour and the different activities in the traditional and modern sectors.

B. Employment in the traditional sector

For the sake of convenience, and because of its relevance to the problem under discussion,[1] we shall refer here to the analytical table of the work force devised by Gerry (*6*) (Table 3); but first a number of remarks are in order.

To begin with, we may note, in agreement with the author, that the categories identified are not "impermeable" or discontinuous. In another context King has shown, by means of a survey of occupational biographies, how a given worker and his family can transit from one situation to another (*16*). Further, we may perfectly easily envisage an infinite number of intermediate categories, between for example the "pure self-employed worker", and "disguised wage employment". The purpose and the significance of distinctions is to illustrate the complexity and the subtle shading of the continuum of the work force.

Secondly, it is worth noting the significance of distinctions for the purpose of discussion. For "direct wage employment" refers to the work force in the modern sector, and to journeymen in the traditional sector—it therefore refers to only a fraction of total wage employment; the "reserve army" does not refer to the same

---

1. Bouquillion-Vaugelade has produced a concrete example of a typology of urban employment, with reference to Pikine-Dakar (see Appendix 2, p. 132).

"population" as in Marx: it represents labour awaiting integration into the modern sector, working alternately in it and in the traditional sector; (is it possible to train the "reserve army"? If so, to enter the modern sector or to maintain it in a transitional state? Is the "reserve army" heading for extinction?). "Disguised wage employment" needs to be distinguished from "pure self-employment". These two categories of labour—the former partly so—correspond to a single status in population census returns: "self-employed". In fact, a close examination of the conditions of production, of the evolution of surplus value, show that "disguised wage employment" (comprising artisans and apprentices belonging to the sub-contracting sector) is "quasi-salaried", and that the only practical differences from salaried employment are of a legal and administrative order (social insurance, tax schedules, etc.). Are we heading for a decline or an expansion of disguised wage employment? And what about pure self-employment? Writing about artisans in African towns, Olivier Lebrun identifies two opposing and concomitant patterns: development and dissolution (*17*). Charmes, in a survey on Tunis, has shown that certain industries—timber and mechanical workshops—are dominated by small-scale production units whose numbers, jobs and development prospects are "self-generated"; that in others—tanneries and textiles—big industry dominates from the point of view of the employment scene, leading to a classical pattern of dissolution of the artisan sector by capitalist industry (*18*). We may readily imagine that the consequences will by no means be the same, depending on whether we are referring to "pure self-employment" or to "disguised wage employment". The decline of sub-contracting activities can have positive effects, such as limiting the extraction of surplus value from the traditional sector, but its effects on employment will be negative (all other things being equal). Conversely, the development of disguised wage employment, which probably occurs to the detriment of "pure self-employment", may be interpreted as a transitional stage on the road towards complete proletarianization of the traditional sector, but may have positive short-term effects even if in the longer run these effects are less predictible. The last category of the work force—which is not really one and which to some extent derives its definition negatively from the others—is the residue, which has grown out of research on marginality in Latin America (*1*):

TABLE 3. Structural analysis of the work force.

Fraction of work force	'Direct' wage employment	Reserve army of labour
GENERAL DESCRIPTION	(1) Workers in capitalist industry (i.e. 'formal sector').	(2) Casual workers in capitalist industry (both permanent and circulating between this and petty commodity production).
LABOUR POWER REPRODUCED VIA	(6) Repititious sale of labour-power in the capitalist production process.	(7) Intermittent sale of labour-power plus some petty commodity production, services, and elements of (10).
OWNERSHIP AND PRODUCTION RELATIONS		
Ownership Maintained	–	–
Production Process Controlled	–	–
Surplus Appropriated By direct Producer	–	–
FUNDAMENTAL LABOUR–CAPITAL RELATIONSHIP	Real subsumption of labour to capital.	Real (but intermittent) subsumption, alternating perhaps with formal subsumption of labour to capital.
GENERAL 'FUNCTIONAL' RELATIONSHIP WITH CAPITALIST MODE OF PRODUCTION	Labour directly 'functional' in capitalist production and accumulation.	Alternating membership of capitalist labour-force as well as 'functional' relative surplus population, according to cycles of capitalist accumulation.

SOURCE C. Gerry (6).

"Disguised" wage employment	'Pure' self employment	Residuum (open unemployed; lumpenproletariat)
(3) Small proprietors and/or their workers with consistent subcontractual and similar relations with capitalist industry.	(4) Small proprietors independent of subcontractual, outworking, etc., relations producing for individual clients or intermediaries.	(5) Unsuccessful sellers/users of labour-power.
(8) Piece-rate "wage" and perhaps elements of (9) (apprentice exploitation in evidence).	(9) Petty commodity production (including some apprentice exploitation) intrafamily transfers.	(10) Combined elements of (6), (7), (8) and (9) but also possibly begging, extorsion, political 'employment', family parasitism, 'illegal transfers.
−/+	+	+/−
−/+	+	+/−
−/+	+	+/−
Formal subsumption of labour to capital on a relatively permanent basis.	Labour-process subordinated to capital in sphere of circulation, no subsumption in sphere of production.	Either minimal relations with capital, or differing degrees of subsumption of labour to 'illegal' capital.
Labour directly 'functional' but also subject to changes according to cycles of capitalist accumulation.	Indirectly 'functional' (provision of wage goods and as back-up battalion to reserve army).	Occasionally 'functional' (politics rather than economics) but more typically 'disfunctional' (disruptive, costly).

this is a highly mixed bunch which includes vagrants, prostitutes, beggars, people living off expedients, what is known as the dangerous class, although it includes ex-able-bodied workers, victims of accidents at work, *déclassés,* the wretched of the earth, etc. This group, characterized by unemployment, very low real earnings, exclusion from civil society, lack of associations and geographical identity, etc., constitutes what McGee calls the proto-proletariat, while according to Quijano it corresponds to the sub-proletariat or, according to other authors, the infra-urban population (*1, 19*). The residue, according to the foregoing table, may be said to have a functional role *vis-à-vis* capital in as much as it contributes to the reproduction of the workforce either through past activities (ex-workers, accident victims, people who have lost their jobs through urban development) or else through present or future illegal activities which help feed and raise children and adolescents who could one day occupy jobs outside the residue.

Thirdly, Gerry's analysis of the structure of the workforce nevertheless raises problems of its own. For instance, it may be noted that all occupational categories are defined essentially in terms of their degree of adequacy or dysfunctionality *vis-à-vis* capital. In other words, these categories are relevant within a functionalist analytical framework and the table is, in a manner of speaking, "capitalocentric", suggesting (whatever the author may claim) that the development of capitalism is going to entail the gradual encroachment of wage employment (modern sector) on "pure self-employment" (traditional sector), thereby more or less condemning the "residue" to ultimate extinction. Incidentally, this view is not entirely incompatible with the generalized (to cover several sectors) dualist models, and the table opposite derived from Steel's (*9*) analysis in three sectors clearly shows this, provided one is prepared to accept the following approximations:
— modern sector by direct wage employment;
— small-scale commodity production and sub-contracting sector by intermediary sector with disguised wage employment and pure self-employment;
— traditional non-commodity sector by casual sector including reserve army and residue.

In practice these correspondences are obviously "short cuts", and not altogether justifiable when we observe (i) the dualist model's neglect of the problem of social relations of production,

TABLE 4. Characteristics of the casual, intermediate and modern sectors.

	Casual	Intermediate	Modern
1. *Barriers to entrance*	Negligible	Medium: fixed capital or human investment	High: substantial investment; economies of scale; legal monopoly
2. *Capital*			
a. value of fixed assets	Negligible	Low, average	High
b. predominant form of capital	Working capital	Physical investment or investment in human capital	Physical (fixed assets)
c. access to institutional capital	None	Low or non-existent	Yes
d. main source of finance	Personal, family	Personal, family	Loans
3. *Labour productivity*			
a. average (output per worker)	Low	Average	High
b. marginal (average additional output per additional worker)	Negligible (owing to surplus labour)	Average	High
4. *Wages*	Income shared	Market wage	Average labour productivity = wages ≥ minimum wage
5. *Employment*[1] (number of workers)	*Individual firm or family*
employees only
No full-time workers	*Handicrafts*
from 1 to 4 workers[2]	*Small-scale production*
5-9, 10-29
Full-time workers	*Average size*
30-49	*Large-scale*
50-99 100+

The divisions given here apply to Africa in general; for other regions, or specific countries, it could be that other divisions would be more appropriate.

1. The divisions given here apply to Africa in general; for other regions, or specific countries, it could be that other divisions would be more appropriate.
2. May be either apprentices or part-time workers, as well as full-time salaried workers.

SOURCE W. Steel(9)

and particularly its neglect of the problem of control over the process of production and the mode of appropriation of surplus, and (ii) the radical model's neglect of the possibilities for expansion of the traditional sector in a development strategy centred not on the supply of production [1] but on the demands of the workers. On the other hand, the two tables can be used to contrast the strengths and weaknesses of the dualist and the radical schools: the former—within an a-historical, one might almost say "instantaneous", framework, based on micro-surveys—remain highly empirical but help to pinpoint the constraints imposed by, and the interactions between, the different factors in economic policy (labour productivity, hourly wage rates, production financing systems); however, they neglect power relations between dominant and dominated social groups; the latter unfortunately tend to stick at a high level of generality not easily tested, but by introducing a certain determinism on the basis of an historical view they do tend to demonstrate both the limitations of partial types of action and the dialectical character of relations between capital and labour. [2]

1. For example, Steel notes, "In a two-sector model, a policy of expanding the demand for workers in the informal sector and of training such workers to increase the supply of them may be effective in fighting unemployment in the following way: a) by reducing the relative size of the modern sector...; b) by preventing informal wages from falling yet further compared with minimum rates in the modern sector, and c) by making experienced workers from the informal sector more attractive to employers in the modern sector. It therefore becomes less worthwhile remaining unemployed, while leaving incentives to emigrate more or less untouched. However, this solution to the problem of unemployment does involve sacrificing a certain amount of output (relative to the expansion of the modern sector) were the informal sector to amount to disguised unemployment" (9). See also (3) and (7).
2. For example, writing about the problem of reproduction of the work force, Hugon says: "The 'informal' sector provides a livelihood for unsalaried workers, constituting a pool of labour available for the requirements of accumulation, thereby playing an essential role in the reproduction of human energies in the towns. The accumulation of capital in societies where regulatory mechanisms are limited and where there is no general social security or welfare system tends to eliminate a portion of the population from the process of reproduction. The 'informal' sector is thus fed by workers arriving from the countryside, having been eliminated from artisan or urban capitalist forms of production; it plays a twofold role of reproduction and devaluation of the work force (41). On the one hand, the capitalist sector requires a large pool of labour owing to the speed at which it wears workers out, to fluctuations in production or to the search for

Having thus briefly, and incompletely, surveyed the theoretical discussion, one is obliged to conclude that we are up against a dead end relieved by a handful of points on which all the different schools of thought agree:

1. The dead end
This refers to the prospects for the development of the traditional sector. (a) For certain people, very broadly, capitalism will develop on the basis of this sector (by extortion of surplus value), thereby condemning it, contradictorily, to extinction (self-employment cannot indefinitely ensure its reproduction by exploiting apprentices and family transfers) and/or preserving itself through expelled workers from the capitalist sector (the accumulation of capital entailing—in societies where the state plays no regulatory role—the visible elimination of workers from the production process, these workers returning to swell the ranks of, or replace, workers in the traditional sector). Consequently, the non-modern sector plays a specific role *vis-à-vis* the modern sector: that of a "breeding-ground, with its own laws of reproduction, which capitalist units draw on as and when needed" (5). The apparent paradox of the rural exodus, which has been going on for 15 or 20 years, of a low rate of creation of salaried jobs without any visible increase in unemployment or poverty, may thus be accounted for. However, a question mark hangs over the future: how far, and for how long, can this process continue, and what can be the role of external agents not explicitly taken into account (such as the State, and changes in the prevailing international economic forces) in the outlook for the future? (b) For others, very broadly, there are no determinisms, and the political authorities have a broad range of options open to them; obviously the earlier (and in some cases still prevailing) *laisser-faire* approach offers no hope of breaking the vicious circle of "unemployment, income inequalities, marginalization of the greater proportion of the human and eco-

---

lower social costs; over the long run it does not assume responsibility for the reproduction of labour power (over the entire length of the life-cycle); small-scale activities do assume a portion of this cost. On the other hand, the non-capitalist sector, by utilizing unremunerated labour time and by this means producing low-cost goods, contributes to the devaluation of labour power where productivity differentials are inferior to differences in the rate of remuneration of labour." (5).

nomic potential, preservation and expansion of the traditional sector, low growth rates". However, it is possible to devise policies that give priority to the fight to eliminate unemployment and poverty on the basis of a stimulatory analysis of the behaviour of the "modern", "intermediate" and "traditional-casual" sectors; and on the basis of a similar analysis of action upon demand rather than upon supply; for example, it has been proposed to redistribute income in favour of those groups in the population having the greatest propensity to buy the products of the traditional-modern sector,[1] since expansion of demand for this sector's products would boost output and shift the demand for labour outwards, thus helping to cut the stock of residual or surplus unemployed or under-employed population; the awkward question remains, obviously, "what kind of growth strategy, how far should the "intermediate" sector spread compared with the modern sector, and is it desirable—at a certain threshold—to sacrifice output for employment? It is technically and politically awkward to answer this question: technically because we know neither the difference between the marginal return on capital in either the modern or the "intermediate" sectors, nor how productivity evolves as the size of these sectors changes; politically, we find ourselves back at square one faced with the problem of accumulation.

2. Points of consensus and facts

The abundant empirical and theoretical work conducted in recent years does however yield a few points of agreement relevant to this paper.

(a) Both dualists and radicals reject dichotomous views expressed in terms of modern/traditional, formal/informal, structured/unstructured, etc., arguing that none of them reflects the actual situation. Whatever the discriminatory criteria used to separate sectors, we are obliged to observe that there is indeed a continuum of situations between, for example, a multinational's subsidiary manufacturing microprocessors, a domestic batik workshop, the street newspaper seller, and the black market currency dealer; and that it is difficult to eliminate arbitrariness in deciding where to draw the line between the traditional sector and the

---

1. Similar to what Steel calls the "intermediate sector".

modern sector. Concerning workers in the different sectors, an additional complication arises out of the fact that the same categories of labour may belong to several sectors (wage-earners, for example), and out of the fact that a single individual may belong either simultaneously or successively to both the modern and the traditional sectors. In the circumstances, if—as we shall in this volume—we continue to speak in "dichotomous terms",[1] we shall be doing so both for the sake of convenience in analysing the problem of growth and employment, and because we implicitly postulate the existence of activities whose characteristics, defined in relation to capital and its accumulation, are distributed in a statistically contrasting manner. In other words, to simplify, the fact of opposing modern and traditional does not rule out the possibility that activities belonging to one sector may also belong to the other (depending on the criteria used), but does imply that the "modal characteristics" are distinctly different when we relate these activities to capital and its accumulation.[2]

(b) As a corollary, it is nowadays agreed that any analysis, any discussion of a sub-set of a country's different spheres of activity (traditional, informal, etc.) is meaningful only when referred to the whole. According to the dualists, for example, wage rates in the urban traditional sector are practically meaningless unless compared with rural wage rates and rates in the modern sector. According to the radicals, it is impossible to analyse the problem of development in the traditional sector without reference to its degree of autonomy *vis-à-vis* the modern capitalist sector.

(c) Granted the difficulty of measuring and comparing partial data, the position of employment in the non-modern sector varies sharply according to the branch of activity concerned. Some examples, which somewhat misleadingly identify self-employment with the non-modern sector, demonstrate this point:

— in Kenya, in 1970, self-employed workers as a percentage of salaried employment varied as follows: 1.8 per cent in the service

---

1. Even when we add the intermediate sector, and/or sub-contracting.
2. Some people are bound to protest energetically at the heavily discriminatory role accorded to capital, and are likely to advance the "mode of production" and its adequacy to the needs of the country as the only acceptable discriminatory criterion. While agreeing with them, we have preferred to employ a more approximate, though more "operational" reference.

sector; 3.5 per cent in the vehicle motor trade; 9,7 per cent in the wholesale trade, and 177.6 per cent in the retail trade (4);
— In the Philippines, in 1971, self-employment expressed as a percentage of wage employment varied between 4 per cent in miscellaneous services, 8.5 per cent in personal services, 33 per cent in transport and communications, and 24 per cent in trade. Data on the activity of unpaid family workers confirm these variations between sectors of activity (1.5 per cent in transport, 20 per cent in personal services, 58 per cent in trade) (8);
— In Abidjan, in 1970, the percentage of workers in the unstructured sector was 12.2 per cent in foodstuffs, 33 per cent in "leathergoods and footwear", 18 per cent in building and public works, 16 per cent in "transport and communications", 66 per cent in trade (7);
— In Brazil, in 1972, self-employment was patterned as follows: 0.3 per cent in the building trade, 2.2 per cent in the professions, 9.3 per cent in the manufacturing industry, 26 per cent in trade, 47.6 per cent in personal services, and 14 per cent in other branches (20);
— In Jakarta, in 1971, self-employment and unpaid family workers accounted for 5 per cent of all jobs in construction and public services, 9.9 per cent in manufacturing industry, 12.7 per cent in transport and communications, 52.6 per cent in farming, and 69 per cent in trade (2);

In Gran Asunción, the informal sector as a proportion of each branch of activity is given in Table 5.

Apart from difficulties connected with the terms used and their definition, these brief examples show beyond doubt that there is no clear-cut general trend as to variations in the place of self-employment from one branch to another.[1] It all depends on the structure of the productive system and the specific context in each city (or country) under consideration. It might be inferred from this that the outlook for the traditional sector is "open", in the sense that we cannot state *a priori* that certain branches ought to be given priority in growth strategies centred on the traditional sector. Besides trade or personal services, informal employment

---

1. Except perhaps in "trade" and "personal services", which are clearly the branches in which the proportion of salaried employment is relatively the lowest.

TABLE 5. Gran Asunción: structure of employment by branch of activity, 1973 (percentages).

Branch of activity	Informal sector	Private formal sector
Industry	59	41
Construction	62	38
Shopkeeping	71	29
Hawkers, street traders	95	5
Banking and financial services	18	82
Basic services	41	59
Domestic service	100	0
Repairs and maintenance	68	32
Other private services	57	43
Others	67	33
In private employment	68	32
Total employment	57	26

SOURCE PREALC, 1973.

could also be expanded in repairs and maintenance, in the building trade, and even in industry. In the language of the economist, activities requiring a low capital input can be found in every branch of the economy. In some cases this will probably take the form of sub-contracting, while in others that of small-scale commodity production of goods and services.

(d) The handful of indirect data we have on the evolution of the traditional sector in the course of time show that the activities of this sector have developed vigorously in certain countries, while in others, on the contrary, employment in the traditional sector has declined (see Table 6).

These patterns are probably due in part to the lack of homogeneity in the figures available; but they probably illustrate also the different development contexts and the contradictory prospects on offer to the traditional sector:

— "sub-contracting": data are scarce; but it is not inconceivable that sub-contracting could develop considerably in certain sectors (clothing, footwear, small mechanical engineering, for example);

— "small-scale commodity production": here, we can expect a twin situation of "dissolution/development", depending on the circumstances. "Restructuring" or capture of a market by a mul-

TABLE 6. Proportion of self-employed (and family) workers in the non-agricultural work force (percentages).

	1960 Census	1970 Census
Argentina	11.7	16.6
Brazil	23.8	20.2
Colombia	22.2	23.1
Chile	18.2	17.9
Mexico	21.3	21.1
Venezuela	22.5	24.3

SOURCE ILO Yearbooks.

tinational firm could cut the ground from under the feet of small-scale producers. But the expansion of needs in the towns, the relative facility of access (low initial capital requirements), and the increased output of experienced apprentices, are all factors that could stimulate the expansion of small-scale commodity production;
— trade and services (including repair workshops): when associated with urban expansion are undoubtedly elements of a burgeoning traditional sector;
— the "residue": by definition it is difficult to assess past development and prospects for the future. The fact that these activities which attract "migrants" act as a kind of "safety-valve" points to the conclusion that the dimensions of the "residue" are bound to swell and shrink in time with fresh influxes and the level of urban employment. However, the few available surveys (including one in Cali, Colombia) tend to show that access to "residual" activities is stringently controlled and suggest that employment in the "residue" is relatively stable.

II. Profiles of workers in the traditional sector

In the previous chapter we proposed to divide the traditional sector into four sub-sectors, each following specific rules and having prospects of its own. Ideally, it would be desirable to study the characteristics of workers in each of these sub-sectors separately in order to identify some specific educational and professional profiles and to draw some conclusions as to development prospects for each and regarding an education or training policy designed for informal employment.

Unfortunately, the results of existing surveys will not permit analysis of this kind. Not all the research so far conducted reviews workers' characteristics systematically. After collecting their data, these analyses—which focus on sectors of activity—are far more concerned to show the intersectorial diversity of workers' profiles than to pinpoint differences within a single sector according to such criteria as the sales of the enterprise, its profits, type of clientèle, and type of link or degree of integration with the modern sector. Moreover, data sources and scope vary greatly from one survey to the next. Some are based on household surveys or existing census data, as in the case of the PREALC studies on Asunción (Paraguay), San Salvador, Quito and Guayaquil (Ecuador), Santo Domingo (Dominican Republic), Mexico, Guadalajara, Monterrey (Mexico) (*1*), Bienefeld's study on Tanzania (*23*) or certain ILO analyses of African, Asian or Latin American cities: Jakarta (*2*), Sao Paulo (*28*), Lagos (*43*). These studies do permit general analysis of workers' profiles in the traditional sector, but provide no link with the enterprises they work in nor any indication of the characteristics and workings of the production units to which they are attached. Other surveys, of an ethno-sociological character, set out to monitor a certain number of enterprises over a certain period of time, and rely chiefly on interviews. These studies, most of which cover Africa, highlight the complexity of relations between the different actors in the traditional sector (entrepreneurs/apprentices), the composition and the dialectical development of this sector, but owing to the limited number of their observations it is impossible to generalize from them: such is the case with the surveys conducted by Devauges (*30*) and Salem (*29*). Lastly, there are the findings of the big ILO statistical surveys of the modernizable traditional sector in five African towns. These have produced a wealth of information on workers' profiles, especially on entrepreneurs' profiles (it is only more recently that attention has turned to the characteristics of apprentices). In particularly we have relied on the findings of Van Dijk's survey of Dakar (*24*) and Ouagadougou (*25*), of Nihan *et al.* on Nouakchott (Mauritania) (*11*) and Lomé (Togo) (*43*). Unfortunately these cover only a handful of branches of activity, those which at first sight have the best chances of developing. They neglect a large proportion of workers in the traditional sector (those in already overcrowded activities and the residual sector jobs) and do not always allow us to make comparisons between worker's profiles in characteristic sub-sectors or in other sectors, including the modern sector.

As can be seen, available data are often incomplete and do not always permit comparison without certain precautions. However, they do reveal a certain number of interesting contrasts within the traditional sector.

1. Contrasts between different categories of worker. Wage-earners or quasi-wage-earners (domestics, apprentices, family workers) have very different characteristics from those of employers or the self-employed in terms of age, migratory status, income. The former constitute a sub-proletariat, a reserve army from among whose number worker/employees are recruited for the modern sector, as well as businessmen for the traditional sector. To a large extent it is the exploitation of the former which enables the traditional sector to survive or even develop, and also permits the relatively high earnings of certain small entrepreneurs.

2. Contrasts between different sectors of activity. Educational background, migratory status and earnings of businessmen vary significantly between, on the one hand, pedlars, domestic services and other personal services, the entire range of activities making up the residue as defined earlier, and on the other hand, shopkeeping, repairs, handicrafts and building. These data also enable us to test a certain number of assumptions that are relevant to our study:

1. *Ease of access to traditional employment.* This is a highly important criterion in describing the workings of the traditional sector. The existing literature very frequently postulates that the traditional sector is very open, concentrating all those who are unable to enter the modern sector: very young workers, or on the contrary very old ones, the illiterate, recent migrants, etc. This would appear to be a simplified view of the situation. For the term informal does not imply that this sector is not governed by certain specific rules regarding its workings and access to it. This is what we shall be trying to show in our analysis of the age, sex, migratory status and ethnic origin of traditional sector workers.

2. *The mode of development of the traditional sector.* Indisputably one of the driving forces behind this sector's growth is the massive influx of migrants in search of work. Not all jobs, however, are directly open to them: while educational background does not appear to be a major obstacle (although this needs checking, owing to the possible consequences this may have on any educational policy designed to foster the traditional sector), it does appear that certain vocational itineraries do enhance a person's chances of one day setting up on his own account. This is what we shall see when we analyse the educational profile, the vocational training and experience of small businessmen.

3. *Relations with the modern sector.* As we have pointed out, existing studies give us no particular clue as to which entrepreneurs maintain what contacts with the modern sector, and will not enable us to study their characteristics. An analysis of the type of vocational training and career history of small entrepreneurs does however enable us to identify those sectors which offer possibilities of transferring to the modern sector (or *vice versa*), possibly thereby facilitating the insertion of workers or control over activities.

A. The age structure of workers

Most existing studies emphasize the extreme youth of employees in the traditional sector. For instance, the PREALC surveys (*1*) show that the under-25s account for 45 per cent of the employed in the traditional sector in the cities of Quito and Guayaquil (Ecuador) as against 19 per cent in urban employment alone. In Mexico (see Table 7), the under-25s account for 51 per cent of traditional sector employees in Mexico City (compared with 38 per cent for the entire working population), 48 per cent in Guadalajara (compared with 39.9 per cent), and 56 per cent in Monterrey (compared with 41.9 per cent). Studies also show that the proportion of old people (over 50) is significant: 14 per cent in Mexico City (as against 13.4 per cent for the entire working population), 18.9 per cent in Guadalajara (against 17.2 per cent) and 14.5 per cent in Monterrey (against 13.2 per cent).

The age-structure differs according to sector. While all sectors employ a high proportion of young people, some employ a higher proportion than others: in Mexico this is particularly the case with repairs and domestic service. Others on the other hand employ a normal proportion of young people but a high proportion of old people, as in trade.

On this point, the case of San Salvador is rather striking. While the under-25s represent 35 per cent of the total working population, they represent no more than 13 per cent of market tradespeople and 19 per cent of street pedlars. On the other hand, one tradesman in five is aged over 55 and 42 per cent are aged over 45. The situation is less clear-cut among street pedlars. [1]

In Santiago de Chili the owner of a commercial enterprise was, on the average, 45 years old in 1969, whilst the average age of the employed population was only 37.

In Cameroon, in small trade, handicrafts and services as a whole, 67.5 per cent of male workers and 69.4 per cent of female workers are aged under 30. But contrary to San Salvador, it is in the services and trade that one comes across the highest proportion of young men, while handicrafts absorbs the greater proportion of old men.

---

1. 26 per cent of them are over 45 (against 20 per cent for the entire working population).

TABLE 7. Mexico: age-distribution of workers in different sectors of informal employment (percentages), 1970.

	Mexico City		Guadalajara		Monterrey	
	<25	>50	<25	>50	<5	>50
Manufacture of foodstuffs	48.8	13.85	45.0	18.72	60.7	10.96
Manufacture of consumer durables and intermediate goods	55.5	9.52	54.2	12.53	53.0	11.34
Clothing	47.6	13.76	52.8	13.37	52.8	13.89
Repairs	66.3	9.88	65.5	10.46	61.9	12.33
Trade	38.2	22.3	38.9	26.5	44.7	23.1
Domestic employment	58.5	9.9	53.0	16.3	65.2	8.7
Total, informal sector	81.1	14.2	48.2	18.9	56.0	14.5
Total, modern sector	30.6	12.9	30.1	15.2	33.3	12.3
Total	38.5	13.4	39.9	17.2	41.9	13.2

SOURCE Sector Informal: Funcionemiento y Politicas. PREALC (*1*).

So far, our analysis has not discriminated between categories: entrepreneurs, workers, apprentices and family workers. With the aid of census figures for a certain number of countries, we can form an idea—even if our analytical categories are still rather rough-and-ready [1]—of age-structure variations according to type of worker.

Appendix tables A.1 and A.2 show that family—unpaid—workers and apprentices are in most cases under 25 years of age. In a detailed survey of some sectors in Abidjan and Yaoundé, Penouil (*26*) has shown that in the garages in Abidjan 79 per cent of supplementary labour (workers and apprentices) consists of people aged under 25 (62 per cent aged under 20), the corresponding figure rising to 90 per cent among tailors in Abidjan, and 91 per cent among Yaoundé carpenters. Additional labour in the traditional sector—which accounts for a fair proportion of jobs in this sector—is thus largely made up of very young

1. Indeed, the categories employer, self-employed worker, family worker, apprentice, etc. as used in censuses do not entirely (nor uniquely) cover the traditional sector. Certain self-employed workers or employers may belong to the modern sector (e.g. members of the professions), whereas certain employees could be regarded as belonging to the traditional sector.

people. Such is by no means the case for employers or self-employed workers. Here we find a fairly high proportion of adults (25-44 years old) as well as older people (45 and over). In particular the proportion of old people is much higher than in salaried employment and in the population as a whole.

Surveys of entrepreneurs show that situations can vary greatly from country to country and from one branch of activity to another.

Surveying urban areas in Tanzania, Bienefeld (23) records the relatively advanced age of self-employed people and employers,[1] sectors with the highest proportion of old people being shops (31 per cent aged over 50), house renting (48 per cent over 50), farming in urban areas, and to a lesser degree construction (18 per cent over 50). The exercise of these different activities presupposes possession of a certain amount of capital and that one has already gained some experience, which is rarely the case for young people. Three sectors are notable for a high proportion of adults (higher, indeed, than in salaried employment): crafts/manufacture (76 per cent aged between 25 and 49, against 50 per cent for the entire population and 58 per cent in salaried employment), the building trade (77 per cent aged 25-49), and hotel or bar manager (72 per cent aged 25-49). There are few activities occupying a high proportion of young people, these being street trading, 31 per cent under 25, which is slightly less however than the corresponding figure for the wage earners (36 per cent). This occupation seems to be the only one which is easily accessible for young people in Tanzania, although it serves also as a refuge for relatively old workers.

In Dakar, in the handicrafts, construction and repairs sectors, the average age of entrepreneurs is relatively high at 39.7 for all sectors together (Van Dijk (24)). As in Tanzania, it appears that the possibility of becoming head of a building contracting firm is reserved for mature or even old men.[2] The same goes for smithies and metalworking (average age: 45.9). Other trades are apparently relatively more open to young people, such as electrical or mechanical repairs (average ages respectively 35.2 and 35.7),

---

1. 23 per cent of them are over 50, compared with only 10 per cent for the entire adult population and 6 per cent of the salaried population.
2. Average age of masons: 46.4 years.

either because they do not necessarily require any initial capital or heavy equipment, or else because it is easier for people who have attained a certain educational level to enter them.

In Lomé [1] entrepreneurs are essentially mature men (Nihan (45)). The young, however, are over-represented in the services (especially in mechanical repairs), while they are under-represented in handicrafts (not a single person under 25 among the metal workers).

In Ouagadougou and Nouakchott the average age of the heads of business interviewed is considerably less: 32 years of age in Ouagadougou and 28 in Nouakchott. Undoubtedly this results from the shape of the pyramid of ages in these two towns. All things being equal, moreover, one notes also that it is in the building trade, artistic crafts, handicrafts that one finds most old businessmen, whereas in the service sector, they are very young (average age: 24 in Nouakchott). [2]

In Abidjan the garage-owners and tailors are young: 39 per cent of the former are under 25 and 58 per cent under 30; 24.7 per cent of the latter are under 25 and 61.9 per cent under 30. Carpenters in Yaoundé are younger still: 52.1 per cent are under 25 and 75.3 per cent under 30. Shopkeepers in the markets, however, are slightly older: only 22.6 per cent of them are under 25, and 31 per cent are over 35. One needs some capital to own a fixed site in the market, which rules out quite a lot of young people.

---

1. 75.8 per cent of the entrepreneurs surveyed were between 25 and 44, 11.8 per cent under 25, and 12.4 per cent over 44.
2. In Ouagadougou (Van Dijk (25)) the young are strongly represented among tailors (average age 27.4, 47.2 per cent aged 25 and under), in transport (average age 28.1, 58 per cent aged under 26), and small trade (average age 27.5, 44.4 per cent aged under 26). In the other sectors one mainly finds a high proportion of adults or even old people, e.g. in the building trade (average age 37.8, 15.3 per cent aged over 50); straw-weavers (average age 39.2); arts and crafts (average age 35.9).

In Nouakchott heads of business are very young. It will be noted, however, that the under-25s age-group is under-represented in handicrafts (10.7 per cent of the work force only) and the building trade (8.1 per cent of the work force). Lastly, the over-45 age-group is under-represented in the services, but far better represented in the construction sector (the only sector containing entrepreneurs aged over 54).

What conclusions can we draw from these figures?

In the first place, the situation varies from country to country, town to town and sector to sector.

Secondly, the great majority of family workers and apprentices are young or very young: this considerably affects the age-profile of the traditional sector, since this category of labour can account for up to 60 and even 75 per cent of informal employment. In Ecuador, for example, 61 per cent of workers in the urban traditional sector are wage-earners (apprentices, domestics and workers). In Mexico, depending on the city, this is the case for between 70.4 and 76.1 per cent of workers. In Dakar 78 per cent of all workers are family workers, journeymen or apprentices, and the corresponding figure for Kumasi is 77 per cent. In the towns of Cameroon 34.3 per cent of people working in the artisan sector and traditional trade are family workers, apprentices or wage-earners (32.8 per cent in handicrafts, 49 per cent in the services, and 32 per cent in trade).

For self-employed workers and employers—the category that most concerns us, either because it is they who are most likely to create new jobs and develop the traditional sector, or because they are better able to earn incomes above the subsistence level—no clear-cut trend is revealed. In certain countries, bearing in mind the urban population's age-structure, they are young, and even very young. Very frequently, however, they tend to be adults and even old. Certain sectors appear to be more difficult of access than others: construction, handicrafts, metalworking, straw-weaving, arts and crafts. Shopkeeping appears more difficult of access in Latin America than in Africa. The services sector is more open everywhere. Young migrants, school leavers, experience a period of unemployment when they arrive on the job market, but eventually find work as family workers, apprentices, traditional sector workers, pedlars, providing small services or working as domestics. In certain cases, if their level of education is sufficiently high, they can rapidly open a repair workshop, but they have little hope of being able to set up quickly on their own account in handicrafts, construction or with a shop or stall in the market before having won their spurs, learning their trade in the employ of another businessmen, or/and without having built up a certain initial capital.

B. Sex distribution of workers in the traditional sector

We have relatively little information about the sex distribution of workers in the traditional sector, because most recent surveys have been devoted to certain sectors of activity only and to men in particular.

To give some idea of the place of women in the traditional sectors of various countries representing different cultures, we have relied on census figures, in spite of the very great imprecision of the categories used and the very approximate character of this approach. Appendix tables A.3 and A.4 give the percentages of women in the non-agricultural working population in a number of countries in Africa, Asia and Latin America.

First of all, it will be observed that the percentage of women in the working population varies greatly from one country to the next. Such variations are due to cultural differences, but they may also stem from different statistical methods used in defining and measuring employment.[1] This specific problem apart, it will be noted that, with a few exceptions (Philippines, Thailand) women account for only a small proportion of the non-agricultural working population: a third at most. However, they are over-represented among family workers in all countries, even when their general level of participation is very low. On the other hand, they are under-represented among employers, accounting for only a very small proportion of people in this category.

Concerning the place of women among the self-employed, several models seem to emerge relative to their position in the modern sector.

Dominant model: in most countries, the proportion of women as self-employed workers is equal and very often superior to that of salaried employees. In other words, they are better represented in the traditional sector than in the modern sector. This is true both in countries that have a high proportion of women in the working population (Philippines, Thailand) and in those with only an average or low proportion of women working. It seems then that the

---

1. In certain countries women are considered as part of the active population only if the work outside the home constitutes their main activity. This probably accounts for the differences between Tunisia and Algeria, for example.

traditional sector is far more open to women than is the modern sector, either because they are not discriminated against as brutally and systematically as in wage employment, or else because working conditions in the traditional sector are particularly suited to women's needs (more flexible working hours and greater opportunities of reconciling family life and child-rearing with paid work), or again because women tend generally to be confined to the least-paid work as family workers first, secondly as self-employed workers, and thirdly in wage employment.

Second model: there is a higher proportion of women in wage employment than among self-employed workers. This is the case in Syria and Egypt, and generally speaking in countries where women account for only a very small proportion of the working population. In these countries, efforts made by the public sector to employ women as teachers, clerks, nurses, etc., enable the modern sector to play a leading role.

Lastly, certain countries with a high proportion of working women, such as Argentina, Costa Rica and Brazil, seem to have a higher proportion of women in wage employment than in self-employment or even among family workers (as is the case with Costa Rica and Brazil). This is probably due to questions of statistical definition, the classification of domestic employment in particular: indeed, a special survey of Sao Paulo (*28*) shows that the traditional sector—defined as all activities in which earnings fall below the minimum wage—employs 54.1 per cent of working women compared with 24.8 per cent of all working men. Similarly, the PREALC surveys of several Latin American cities (*1*) contend that if we take domestic employment into account, (i) the very great majority of women is employed in the traditional sector; (ii) women outnumber men in this sector.

In order to really appreciate the rôle of women in the traditional sector, it is necessary to analyse what types of activity most of them are engaged in:

— census figures show that the bulk of female family workers are employed in trade and services. Self-employed women are chiefly engaged in trade, followed by handicrafts (mainly textiles and clothing) and in the services;

— a survey of handicrafts and small trade in Western Cameroon in 1964-65, cited by IEDES (*7*), shows that in the towns men account for the very great majority of people working in handi-

crafts (82.7 per cent), services (74.4 per cent) and small trade (74.1 per cent). However, in certain specific activities they are outnumbered by women (catering), while in others women are virtually in the majority (tailoring, and trade in food produce);
— in Ouagadougou (25) women account for only 13.5 per cent of the sample of entrepreneurs analysed. They are heavily concentrated in a single sector: weaving, where they account for 62 per cent of the sample; this sector is followed by arts and crafts (19 per cent of the sample), and trade (16 per cent). These are, in general, saturated, declining, activities;
— in San Salvador, 63 per cent of working women are employed in the traditional sector (compared with 29 per cent of men), but of these 63 per cent more than half work as domestics. (If we exclude domestic service, 31 per cent of women work in the traditional sector, compared with 28 per cent of men). Apart from domestic service, these women work in trade: 90 per cent of sales assistants are women;
— in Mexico City,[1] women are chiefly employed in a few sectors: (i) domestic service, (ii) clothing, (iii) trade and selling of food (iv) processing of foodstuffs.[2] They are virtually absent in other sectors: production of consumer goods other than food, repairs, etc. (see Table 8).

On the whole, whether they outnumber men in the traditional sector or not, women tend to be employed in activities which are considered as female, differing little, in the final analysis, from those which are reserved for them in the modern sector: catering, tailoring, clothing (activities similar to domestic tasks), small trade in foodstuffs, domestic service. Apart from trade, these are all activities requiring little in the way of qualifications, little apprenticeship other than family training, and above all they are low-paid activities. On the criterion of women's participation, the

1. Women account for 62 per cent of employment in the traditional sector (Guadalajara: 50.8 per cent; Monterrey: 56.6 per cent), but if we eliminate domestic service they represent only 36.7 per cent (Guadalajara: 37.3 per cent, Monterrey: 31.7 per cent).
2. 67 per cent of women are employed in domestic service (where they account for 95 per cent of the workers), 20.5 per cent in the trade and selling of food (where they account for 43 per cent of the workers), 8.7 per cent in the clothing industry (58 per cent of employment in the sector), 4.1 per cent in the processing of food-stuffs (30 per cent of the sector).

TABLE 8. Percentage of women employed in different sectors, Mexico, 1970.

	Mexico City		Guadalajara		Monterrey	
	Modern sector	Traditional sector	Modern sector	Traditional sector	Modern sector	Traditional sector
Including domestics	23.7	62.25	19.47	50.82	19.35	56.62
Excluding domestics	22.47	36.67	18.55	37.32	18.21	31.74

SOURCE PREALC (*1*).

traditional sector is undoubtedly more open and more flexible than the modern sector, but it is not without well-established rules of its own.

C. Ethnic and family occupational background of workers in the traditional sector

Anyone who has spent any time in Asia and Africa will be aware of the role played by ethnic orgin in the exercise of certain trades. The place of certain castes in India, of the Indians in East Africa, the Chinese in Malaysia and Indonesia, the Bamilekes in Cameroon or the Sarakoles in Mali, etc., is well enough known. Several studies have stressed this point. According to O. Lebrun (*17*), "there does exist a certain specialization in handicrafts based on ethnic groups. Certain groups exercise occupations in which others do not engage. Traditionally handicrafts, outside certain activities such as weaving, are organized along caste lines... most trades have their specific caste, their own rules and rites. Trades are handed down from father to son".

Empirical data is scarce, however, either because the statistical survey did not yield satisfactorily to this kind of analysis (which requires more detailed study of a more anthropological nature), or else because the information obtained may not always be reliable.

Bienefeld, in Tanzania (*23*), notes that non-Africans (Asians and Arabs), play a special role in the traditional sector, even if they account for only 15.5 per cent of the self-employed (against 10 per cent of the total adult population); on the one hand they constitute the majority of tradespeople, and on the other 42 per cent of them work in the traditional sector (compared to only 24 per cent of Africans).

In Nouakchott (*11*), only 54.2 per cent of businessmen are Mauritanians (50 per cent in manufacturing, 39.5 per cent in services, 75.7 per cent in the building trade). Foreigners, Senegalese in particular, dominate the service sector (52.6 per cent) and play a very important role in handicrafts (38.9 per cent).

A study of the Senegalese commercial system conducted in France (Salem (*29*)) shows that two groups control the whole of this system: Laobe artisans, an ancient Peuhl caste of dry-coopers, and a group of tradespeople, mainly Wolof, whose cohesion depends essentially on membership of the religious brotherhood of the Mourides. The author concludes "one cannot discuss problems relating to the future of the informal sector without taking into account their organizational and ideological backbone. Family/ethnic/religious/economic groups arise and define themselves, and then reform, in the towns. It is by analysing the use and the reinterpretation of the rules governing the lives of these groups that we can gain insight into the disappearance of some and the emergence of others. The urban economy is therefore perhaps not quite as informal as is claimed or as it makes itself out to be."

In the absence of better knowledge of the extent of trade specialization among ethnic groups, we do at least have some knowledge of the process by which it develops, in particular through the apprenticeship system. In fact it is from the family (in the broad sense of the word) of the head of business that apprentices are most often recruited.[1] This results from the fact that the apprenticeship contract entails obligations on both sides. Devauges observes that in the Congo "the condition of any such traditional alliance is based essentially on apprentice and master

---

1. In Abidjan and Yaoundé a substantial proportion of apprentices belong to the family of the head of the enterprise: 61 per cent in the case of garages, 59 per cent for tailors, and 44 per cent for carpenters. In Dakar 25 per cent of employees are related to the head of the enterprise (from 7 per cent among watch-repairmen to 31 per cent among brickmakers and 30 per cent among blacksmiths and metalworkers—existence of a caste of blacksmiths). In Lomé 23 per cent of apprentices are related to the head of the enterprises surveyed, the exact figure varying from 13.4 per cent in construction to 34 per cent in handicrafts.

belonging to the same ethnic group" (*30*). We shall see later the importance of apprenticeship in the preservation and development of the traditional sector in Africa. Suffice it to stress here the fact that the economic and social organization of this sector is based on the transmission, and possibly the exploitation, of qualifications through the extended family in a manner compatible with traditional patterns of solidarity.

It may also prove worth while to analyse the family and occuptional backgrounds of the heads of businesses, and particularly their parents' occupations. The only information we have concerns Nouakchott, Dakar, Lomé and Ouagadougou. In Nouakchott, the parents of entrepreneurs were either farmers-fishermen-stockbreeders (47.6 per cent), tradespeople (13.1 per cent), or artisans (16.2 per cent). Bearing in mind the structure of the working population in Mauritania, the sons of modern sector employees (civil servants in particular) and of tradespeople and artisans are very heavily over-represented among heads of businesses. In Ouagadougou the heads of businesses surveyed are chiefly peasants' sons (64 per cent), sons of artisans and tradespeople (24.3 per cent), and much less often sons of workers and employees in the modern sector (4.3 per cent); traditional handicrafts are apparently handed down from father to son (artistic artisans: 59 per cent sons of artisans, tradespeople and batik producers; 31 per cent sons of artisan tradesmen), whereas the more modern activities are exercised by the sons of peasants (building trade 73 per cent, small services 75 per cent—14 per cent of the latter are exercised by sons of employees in the modern sector). In Lomé 73.6 per cent of businessmen surveyed (Nihan (*43*)) are sons of peasants. It is interesting to note, however, that in certain of the most dynamic sectors the proportion of civil servants' sons is particularly high: 33.3 per cent of electrical repairers and 25 per cent of building contractors; this is true for only 1.5 per cent of all heads of businesses. In Dakar, according to a study conducted by BREDA, fathers' occupations were as shown in Table 9.

There is a high proportion of sons of artisans/tradespeople and sons of civil servants among artisans in the Medina (whose income is generally considerably superior to incomes in the Grand Yoff). It is also noteworthy that modern artisans are rarely sons of traditional artisans but are far more likely to be sons of modern artisans themselves.

TABLE 9. Father's occupation, Dakar (percentages).

	Medina artisans (metal and timber joiners and masons)	Grand Yoff artisans (timber joiners, masons, painters, moulders)
Artisan	34	12
Tradesman	3	6
Civil servant	10	—
Peasant	40	71
Others	13	—
Total	100	100

SOURCE Françoise Durand, «Les Cars rapides à Dakar» (IEDES doctoral thesis).

These few figures suggest that being the son of a traditional sector businessman may, to begin with, be a considerable advantage in gaining access to and succeeding in the same sector (both in financial terms and as regards learning the trade and familiarizing oneself with the milieu), and next that the relations between the modern sector and the traditional sector are complex and varied: the fact that a by no means negligible proportion of civil servants' sons have set up in business on their own account leads one to suppose that for certain members of the civil service (or of the modern sector in general) investing in the traditional sector can be a highly profitable business.

D. The place of migrants in the traditional sector

Migrants play a very important role in the growth of the traditional sector, since it is in this sector that most of them find employment on their arrival in town.[1] It is interesting though to analyse, in greater detail, the process whereby they are integrated. This may vary from one country to another.

In San Salvador, for instance, recent migrants (arrived less than a year ago) are distributed among the different sectors as follows:

---

1. 82 per cent in Gran Asunción, 69 per cent in San Salvador.

55 per cent in domestic service, 14 per cent in the non-domestic traditional sector, and 31 per cent in the modern sector. After a few years, the situation alters: 50 per cent of migrants resident for over ten years now work in the modern sector, 34 per cent in the non-domestic traditional sector, while only 16 per cent are domestic servants. By comparison, 61 per cent of native towndwellers work in the modern sector, a smaller proportion (31 per cent) works in the non-domestic traditional sector, and a negligible proportion in domestic service (see Table 10). The authors of the PREALC survey account for this difference in migrants' occupations depending on length of residence in the city by the fact that migration into San Salvador has slowed down over the past five years: those activities in the traditional sector which absorbed a high proportion of migrant labour in the past have gradually become saturated, leaving new arrivals no alternative but domestic service. However, this distribution probably also reflects another phenomenon, and in particular a distinct change in migrants' occupations: after a number of years in the city a range of opportunities of employment in the modern sector or the non-domestic traditional sector become available to them. On arrival in the city, migrants accept any job offered them, essentially ones requiring no particular experience. Thus women find jobs as servants while men find a job that just about enables them to survive, or else accept occasional work in the traditional or modern sector; only very rarely can they set up on their own account or become apprentice-workmen in the traditional sector. After some years in town, women abandon domestic service in favour of a job in the traditional or modern sector—which gives them slightly superior status, even if working conditions are scarcely better. Men, having acquired some know-how and a certain amount of experience, tend to set up in business on their own account or to become workers in the modern sector. But this is not to say that the traditional sector is nothing but a kind of anteroom to the modern sector, for after ten years' residence in town 50 per cent of migrants still work in that sector. The situation is therefore much more complex, since there exist different kinds of occupation within the traditional sector itself.

The findings of a survey on Sao Paulo (Kalmane Schaefer (28)) would seem to confirm this hypothesis: the likelihood of working in the traditional sector is the higher the briefer the person's resi-

TABLE 10. San Salvador: occupational profile of migrants by length of stay, 1974.

	Migrants: length of stay in years				Non-migrants	Total
	0-1	2-5	6-9	10 & over		
Traditional sector						
Non-domestic	14	26	32	34	31	31
Domestic	55	29	22	16	8	16
Modern sector	31	45	46	50	61	53
Total	100	100	100	100	100	100

SOURCE PREALC (*1*).

dence in town. Conversely, the longer the person's stay in the city the greater are the opportunities of transferring to the modern sector. Certain migrants (women especially) remain in the traditional sector, but their occupations evolve. Thus 39.4 per cent of recent male migrants work in the traditional sector, and this proportion declines among groups that have lived longer in the city, dropping to 26.4 per cent among migrants with more than six years' residence, and to 20.8 per cent among non-migrants. Parallel to this, the proportion of men working in construction falls, whereas the proportion of those in mechanical repairs etc. and trade increases. 73 per cent of women newly-arrived in Sao Paulo work in the traditional sector. Among those with more than six years' residence in the city this proportion falls to 59.5 per cent, and one also observes a complete change of occupation: in particular many of them quit domestic service in favour of trade, clothing, health activities, etc.

In Africa, migrants make up the bulk of labour employed in the traditional sector. This is accounted for by the relatively recent development of the towns. Thus, only 7 out of the 298 entrepreneurs interviewed in Kumasi, or 2.2 per cent of those interviewed in Nouakchott, were in fact born and raised in the city itself. Leaving aside these rather obvious cases, it appears that migrants are often better represented among workers in the traditional sector, self-employed and small entrepreneurs, than among employees in the modern sector or in the population as a whole.[1]

In Dakar the percentage of recent migrants is relatively low compared to other African towns (Table 11): only 7.7 per cent of entrepreneurs interviewed had been in the city for less than five years, and 21.8 per cent for less than ten years. This last figure is comparable with the proportion of migrants having arrived in the city less than ten years ago in the urban population as a whole, according to the 1970 census: Dakar is an older city; if however we take into account the substantial influx of migrants after the drought in 1970 it is reasonable to assume that migrants are under-represented in the activities surveyed. The survey covered handicrafts and repairs, which are probably not activities in which fresh arrivals can easily set up on their own account: it is likely that other activities more easily lend themselves to the role of "soaking up" these new migrants: pedlars, small personal services, apprenticeship, or even unemployment. This would need checking.

What in fact we find is a very broad variety of possibilities of absorption for migrants.

Certain sectors seem relatively accessible to migrants. Such is the case with watchmaking, electrical repairs, timber joinery and moulders: most heads of business have been in town for under 20 years. Other sectors, on the other hand, seem more difficult to get into for people not born in town or who have not been there many years. This is the case with masonry (70.3 per cent of employers were either born in Dakar or have lived there for over 20 years); the situation is similar, though less marked, in metal joinery, mechanical repairs and upholstery. Is it because these are longstanding trades in Dakar and declining relatively?

Tanzania provides another example illustrating the dificulties preventing the integration of migrants in certain activites in the traditional sector (Bienefeld (23)): they account for 76 per cent of all wage-earners and 67 per cent of the total urban population, but

1. In Ouagadougou 22 per cent of traditional entrepreneurs have lived in the city for less than five years and 43 per cent for less than ten years. In Abidjan 25 per cent of garage-owners and 39 per cent of tailors arrived less than five years ago (Penouil (26)). Most of them have been in the city for fewer than twenty years. In Yaoundé 25 per cent of entrepreneurs arrived less than six years ago.

TABLE 11. Dakar: distribution of heads of business by length of residence in city and sector of activity, 1977.

	All sectors	Metal joinery	Timber joinery	Electrical repairs	Mechanical repairs	Moulder	Mason	Upholsterer	Watchmaker
Percentage born in Dakar	23.7	17.9	18.9	17.0	36.4	15.7	29.6	24.4	6.8
Percentage residing in Dakar for over 20 years	29.7	39.7	31.0	23.4	20.4	26.3	40.7	26.7	29.5
Sub-total	53,4	57,6	49,9	40,4	56,4	42,0	70,3	51,1	36,3
Percentage residing in Dakar for less than 5 years	7.7	7.6	8.1	8.5	6.8	5.3	3.7	6.6	13.6

SOURCE Van Dijk. *Enquête sur le secteur non-structuré* (Survey of the unstructured sector). Dakar. ILO *(24)*.

are under-represented everywhere except in handicrafts, bars and hotels. Thus, while street trading appears to be a wide-open activity, calling for no special preparation, migrants are under-represented in it; Bienefeld explains this phenomenon by the need for contacts with local sources of supply.

McGee (27) curiously, observes the same phenomenon in South-east Asia: it seems that in most south-east Asian countries (except Indonesia) there is a well-established community of hawkers and pedlars which includes a high proportion of native town-dwellers.

To sum up, it seems that the traditional sector absorbs a very high proportion of new migrants: indeed the influx of jobless people arriving from the country or secondary towns seems to be the main driving force behind the expansion of this sector; however, migrants do not enjoy direct access to all the activities in the traditional sector: in Latin America they tend to start off in domestic service or occasional work. In Africa they are more likely to find work as an apprentice or unskilled worker so as to be able to set up on their own account later on. Even occupations regarded as wide open (pedlar) are not always so. The barriers are apparently of a financial order (the need for a small initial outlay), and ethnic origin. It would be interesting to see whether education or vocational training may constitute an obstacle.

E. Education

One characteristic common to workers in the traditional sector in all countries seems to be their particularly low level of education compared with workers in the modern sector. It is as if, unable to find employment in the modern sector, the least-educated, the illiterates and school drop-outs had no alternative but to seek employment in the traditional sector.

In Gran Asunción (Paraguay) and in the three principal towns of Mexico the traditional sector is by far the biggest employer of functional illiterates.[1] One observes, however, certain variations in

---

1. In Gran Asunción 78 per cent of those who have had three years or less of schooling work in the traditional sector, whereas this percentage falls to 69 for those with four or six years of schooling, 19 for those with ten to twelve years of schooling, and 8 for those with a university education. Domestic service

workers' profiles, according to the branch of activity and the work which they do. Thus in Mexico the highest proportion of functional illiterates is to be found among domestics (70 per cent), producers of foodstuffs (54 per cent) and tradespeople. Electrical and mechanical repairers have an educational level which is higher, since one finds only 19 to 25 per cent functional illiterates in these occupations. Perhaps it is preferable to have a certain minimum education for this kind of work, and indeed one does find a fairly high proportion of young men with a secondary education in these jobs. In San Salvador the educational level of tradespeople is particularly low: 78 per cent of them are functional illiterates with less than four years' elementary education. It should however be noted that there exists a hierarchy as between market shopkeepers and street pedlars: the educational level of the latter is lower still, with 55 per cent fully illiterate and 84 per cent functionally illiterate.

In Africa the educational level of heads of businesses also is very low. In Nigeria, 64 per cent of artisans and owners of small manufacturing establishments in Ibadan had in 1961 received no formal instruction, and only 21 per cent had received a complete primary education or beyond (Callaway (*39*)). These figures should be set alongside the findings of another survey, conducted in 1965, on people employing an average of over 20 workers in Nigeria (*40*): 12.7 per cent had never been to school, 74 per cent had their school-leavers' certificate or better (including 39.2 per cent with a General Certificate of Education or better). The educational level in the traditional sector is therefore much inferior to that of the modern or semi-modern sector.

In Tanzania, 71 per cent of self-employed workers had less than 4 years' schooling. This percentage varies from 80 for street pedlars, who are the least educated of all, to 52 for bar and hotel keepers and 56 for shopkeepers, and rises again to 63 for artisans. Here too there is a notable difference between the educational

---

alone provides employment for 31 per cent of functional illiterates (those with less than four years' education).

The figures are not so high in Mexico City, since the traditional sector employs only 55.2 per cent of all functional illiterates, but in Guadalajara the percentage rises to 65.5. Generally speaking, 56.5 per cent of workers in the traditional sector have had less than four years' education (59 per cent in Guadalajara, 43 per cent in Monterrey).

TABLE 12. Educational background of heads of businesses: results of some surveys.

	Illiterate or no education	Literate and/or Koranic education	Elementary or general education	Intermediate education	Technical education	Secondary education	Other
DAKAR (1977)							
All sectors	12.8	54.8	20.8		11.6		
Metalwork	26.9	55.3	10.2		7.6		
Carpentry	8.1	54.1	18.9		18.9		
Furniture-maker	13.3	49.1	28.8		8.8		
Brickmaker	15.7	63.3	10.5		10.5		
Mason	7.4	55.6	24.1		12.9		
Electrical repairs	11.4	78.1	2.5		8.0		
Mechanical repairs	4.2	38.5	36.1		21.2		
Watch repairs	11.4	70.4	11.4		6.8		
OUGADOUGOU (1976)							
All sectors	47.7	21.7	26.3			4.0	0.3
Arts and crafts	35.1	21.6	40.5			2.7	
Tailor	16.6	22.2	61.1				
Weaver	59.5	19.0	16.7			4.8	
Furniture-maker	19.2	30.6	42.3			3.8	
Construction	61.5	30.7	7.7				
Small scale services	41.6	16.5	27.7			13.8	
Trade	53.4	23.3	16.3			7.0	
NOUAKCHOTT (1977)							
All sectors	22.1	31.2	34.4			12.3	
Production	32.1	26.8	33.9			7.2	
Construction	8.1	45.9	21.7			24.3	
Services	21.1	23.5	47.2			8.2	

Profiles of workers in the traditional sector

KUMASI (GHANA) (1975)			
All sectors	27.5	57.8	2.0
LOME (1978)			
All sectors	25.0	12.7	55.6
Production (timber)	35.5		40.8
Production (metal)	42.9		42.9
Journeyman (construction)	16.7		50.0
Craftsman (construction)	4.2		75.0
Small-scale mechanical	35.3		58.8
Electrical repairs			72.7
Mechanical repairs	21.2		65.9

	5.4
	4.3
	16.7
	18.1
	3.6

SOURCE Van Dijk (24)(25), Nihan (11)(45), Arye (22).

59

level of workers in the traditional sector and those in the modern sector; the percentage of people having had less than 4 years' education in the formal sector is in fact 41, and in the total adult population 52.

Are we to attribute variations between the sectors to different qualification requirements or to other factors? It is intersting, in this respect, to compare these findings with other surveys.

Table 12 summarizes the findings of the surveys conducted in Dakar, Ouagadougou, Nouakchott, Kumasi and Lomé. In four cities the percentage of illiterate entrepreneurs or who have had no other education than the Koranic school or a few literacy classes is very high: Dakar, 67.6; Ouagadougou, 69.4; Nouakchott, 53.3; and Lomé, 38.9. To illustrate these variations according to sector of activity we shall now examine some examples:

(a) *Construction industry*
In Dakar the educational profile of masons differs little from that of the rest of entrepreneurs: at best one finds a slightly higher proportion of masons having attended a few years' general or technical schooling. In Nouakchott building contractors stand out for the high proportion of their number having attended secondary education and the low proportion of illiterates. The same goes for Lomé—with the exception of journeymen. In Ouagadougou, on the other hand, it is in the construction industry that one finds the highest proportion of illiterates and the lowest proportion of people having attended some years of elementary education: 92.2 per cent of building contractors have no education other than the Koranic school or a few literacy classes.

(b) *Services sector*
In Nouakchott a higher proportion of entrepreneurs in service (mechanical and electrical repairs) than in any other kind of activity seems to have attended elementary education (47.2 per cent). Furthermore, in this sector one comes across a lower proportion "of people having attended literacy classes and the Koranic school", but a few secondary-school graduates also.

In Ouagadougou the small services sector (which includes repairs) stands out by the high proportion of secondary-school graduates: 13.8 per cent.

In Lomé electrical repairers are by far the best educated of the employers surveyed. Conversely, in small mechanical engineering one finds a high proportion of illiterates.

In Dakar mechanical repairers have a relatively low level of education, (78 per cent of them have attended only the Koranic school), while in electrical repairs one finds a high proportion of people having attended eiher general education or technical education.

(c) *Manufacturing*

Compared with the other cities, Nouakchott and Lomé contain a high proportion of illiterates and far fewer secondary-school graduates in this sector. In Ouagadougou tailors, artistic craftsmen and furniture makers are relatively better educated than the others, with in particular a high proportion of primary school graduates (respectively 40.5, 61.1, and 42.3 per cent). Straw-weavers and weavers, on the other hand, have a very low educational level. In Dakar the educational level of metalworkers is weak, whereas that of carpenters and furniture-makers is equivalent to the average for businessmen as a whole.

What emerges from these examples is that there is no clear-cut tendency from one country to the next regarding entry qualifications for the different occupations. The most we can say is that it seems as if electrical repairers are in all cases better qualified than the rest. But this is not the case for mechanical repairers, for example. On the other hand, the traditional claim that building and trade require little in the way of qualifications is not borne out in every case.

These variations probably stem from the fact that while the educational profile of different occupations is influenced by different qualification requirements [1] it is also highly influenced by age and sex profiles, ethnic membership and migratory status. In Dakar, the best-educated workers are those born in the city itself, and we have already seen that they are very well represented in the building trade. [2] In Tanzania tradespeople and proprietors of bars and hotels seem to be better educated, but it also happens to be in these occupations that one finds the highest proportion of

---

1. We shall see later that qualifications for the traditional sector are not necessarily acquired through the formal education system.
2. Even if migrants are better educated than the general rural population, they still tend to be less well educated than people born in the towns.

TABLE 13. Kumasi: Educational profiles of businessmen according to age (percentages), 1975.

	Total	20-25	26-30	36-40	46-50	61 and over
No education	27.5	6.8	16.3	55.2	73.3	100
Primary education	12.7	12.3	12.8	3.4	6.7	—
Middle school education	57.7	79.5	68.6	37.9	13.3	—
Technical education	2.0	1.4	2.3	3.4	6.7	—
Total	100	100	100	100	100	100

SOURCE Arye (22)

Asians, whose school attendance rates have always been higher. In Ouagadougou weavers have a poor educational level, but it is also in this occupation that one finds the highest proportion of women. Lastly, the age profile has a considerable influence on educational profile, as can be seen from Table 13 referring to Kumasi.

The younger the businessmen, the greater the proportion of school graduates among their number: the percentage rises from 13.3 among the 46-50s to 79.5 among the 20-25s. Conversely, the percentage of people with no education declines from 73.3 among the 46-50s to 6.8 among the 20-25s. This very accurately reflects the explosion that has occurred in the Ghanaian school system in the last 10-15 years. The rising educational level of traditional workers merely reflects the general rise in the educational level of the population as a whole.

It seems then that education is only very rarely a criterion of access to the traditional sector. It is quite likely, on the contrary, that the first consequence of the arrival of young certificate-holding school-leavers onto the labour market is to squeeze unqualified people out of the modern sector, obliging them to look for work in the traditional sector. It is only when the modern sector has "absorbed its fill" of educated people, in particular by raising the educational standards required for recruitment to different posts, that the rise in the general educational level of the population can begin to make itself felt on the population in the traditional sector. This hypothesis needs to be verified: we would need to be able to compare systematically the educational level of entrepreneurs in the traditional sector with that of the entire urban working population, as has been done by Bienefeld in Tanzania. Unfortunately we lack the data to do so for the time being.

Certain studies have shown that there may be significant differences between the educational level of apprentices and that of employers. In Nouakchott, for example, 79.6 per cent of apprentices and 69.7 per cent of unskilled workers have received no education, which is the case for only 22 per cent of entrepreneurs (see Appendix Table A.5).

In Lomé the difference is less marked, but here too businessmen are better educated than are apprentices (25 per cent illiterates, compared with 36 per cent). Permanent workers have by far the lowest educational level (56.5 per cent illiterates).

What this in fact means is that educational level is not a criterion for indenture as an apprentice or rather that it is a negative criterion where entrepreneurs are seeking very cheap labour—but that it can facilitate the switch-over to becoming self-employed.

While education is not in itself a criterion of access to the traditional sector, it is interesting to analyse the way people acquire the know-how and experience needed for work in the traditional sector.

(d) *Vocational training of entrepreneurs*

Very few entrepreneurs have received any formal vocational training. Surveys of Dakar, Ouagadougou, Nouakchott, Kumasi and Lomé show that only very rarely have more than 10 per cent of them received a formal vocational training, whether in the form of short or long courses, or even correspondence courses (see Table 14).[1] Here, too, analysis sector by sector reveals a certain hetero-

1. The percentage is highest in Dakar, with 11.4 per cent of all those interviewed having received some sort of training (the figure varies from 21.3 per cent for electrical repairers to 7.7 per cent for metalworkers and 6.9 per cent for watch-repairmen and mechanical repairers). In Ouagadougou only 8 per cent of those interviewed have undergone training (19.5 per cent for small services, 3.8 per cent for furniture-making, and 2.4 per cent for trade). In Nouakchott an average of 4.6 per cent of those interviewed have undergone training in a vocational institute (the highest proportion, 8.2 per cent, is to be found in the building trade). In Kumasi and Lomé respectively only 3.4 and 2.6 per cent of those interviewed had received any training in a vocational training centre.

TABLE 14. Vocational training and experience of heads of businesses in the traditional sector (percentages).

	No vocational training	Former traditional sector apprentices	Former modern sector apprentices	Former traditional sector workers	Former modern sector workers	Trained in vocational training centre	Without vocational training in some institutions
DAKAR (1977)							
All sectors	88.6	40.0		17.9	36.1		
Metalwork	92.3	35.8		15.3	34.6		
Carpentry	81.1	25.6		14.9	52.7		
Furniture-maker	91.1	44.4		37.7	17.7		
Brickmaker	89.4	52.6		21.0	21.0		
Mason	87.0	14.8		18.5	64.8		
Electrical repairs	78.7	51.0		6.3	36.1		
Mechanical repairs	93.2	37.5		23.8	35.2		
Watch repairs	93.5	77.2		9.0	11.3		
OUGADOUGOU (1976)							
All sectors	92.0	60.0			10.0		
Arts and crafts	89.2	91.9			2.7		
Tailor	88.8	88.9			8.7		
Weaver	90.4	54.8			0.0		
Furniture-maker	96.2	100.0			30.7		
Construction	96.1	34.7			26.9		
Small scale services	80.5	80.6			11.2		
Trade	97.6	41.9			9.4		
NOUAKCHOTT (1977)							
All sectors	95.4	58.0		25.2			
Production	98.2	65.3		23.2			

Profiles of workers in the traditional sector

Construction	91.8	21.6	48.6
Services	94.7	84.2	5.3
KUMASI (GHANA) (1975)			
All sectors	90.3		5.0
LOME (1978)			
All sectors		88.4	0.9
Production (timber)		96.7	1.1
Production (metal)		95.2	4.8
Journeyman (construction)		100.0	
Craftsman (construction)		91.6	4.2
Small-scale mechanical		100.0	
Electrical repairs		81.8	9.2
Mechanical repairs			9.1

SOURCE Van Dijk (24) (25), Nihan (11) (45), Arye (22)

geneity between the different countries. In Lomé the activities containing the highest proportion of people with a vocational training are, first, electrical repairs, followed by metalwork and construction. In Dakar too electrical repairs ranks top, followed by carpenters, masons and brickmakers; in the three last-named this refers to classes given in a training centre, the Lycée Delafosse, while for the former (electrical repairs) the training in question mainly involves correspondence courses. In Ouagadougou small services are by far the heaviest employers of people with vocational training (this includes electrical repairs), followed by clothing (tailors), and arts and crafts; construction here requires very little in the way of vocational training. Lastly, in Nouakchott construction comes first, followed by services, in their demand for trained personnel, while the manufacturing sectors employ very little. What we observed for general education is here confirmed with respect to vocational training: the general level is very low, but certain service activities such as electrical repairs seem to demand a minimum of education and vocational training. Building, on the other hand, seems to make different demands in Dakar, Lomé or Nouakchott, on the one hand, and in Ouagadougou on the other. The probable explanation of this phenomenon lies in the different ways this sector is organized and its greater or lesser integration into the modern sector.

The small number of people in the traditional sector having attended organized vocational training results undoubtedly from the low level of development of this type of training in these countries, and from the fact that until now it has been open only to people already having a certain basic education: in Kumasi, for instance, the educational profile of employers having undergone training in an institution is distinctly superior to that of other employers: 90 per cent have attended middle school at least (against 59.7 per cent for all employers) and 40 per cent have already attended technical school (see Appendix Table A.6). But this is probably also due to the place and the particular role played by on-the-job training.[1] For apprenticeship plays a very important

---

1. We lack data on the vocational training of workers in the traditional sector in Latin America: it would be interesting though to measure the results of the work done by the SENA (Columbia), INACAP (Chile), INCE (Venezuela), etc.

role and would appear to be the main source of training and of access to the traditional sector in a good many countries. In Kumasi 90.3 per cent of those interviewed had learnt their trade as apprentices in the traditional sector; in Ouagadougou this was the case for 60 per cent of entrepreneurs and for 88.4 per cent of them at Lomé. In Nouakchott 58 per cent of entrepreneurs had been apprentices in the traditional sector and 25 per cent in the modern sector. In a survey on occasional workers in Dakar, O. Lebrun and C. Gerry note that vocational training mainly occurs in the employ of somebody else: out of 285 manufacturers and small artisans, 70 per cent had been apprentices. In Abidjan, de Miras (38) points out: "all those who have now set up on their own account as carpenters, mechanics or tailors have undergone apprenticeship in the trade they now exercise".

It might be thought that the role of apprenticeship declines as the educational level of the people concerned rises, on the one hand, and as vocational training classes are organized on the other. The survey of Kumasi does not bear this out: the proportion of employers having undergone apprenticeship in the traditional sector varies little with age; indeed it is higher among the under-30s (90-93 per cent), despite their higher educational level,

TABLE 15. Kumasi, Ghana: type of vocational training received by entrepreneurs according to age (percentages), 1975.

	20-25	26-30	31-35	36-40	41-45	46-50	51 and over
Training in an institution	6.8	1.2	1.9	3.4	4.8	6.7	0.0
Apprenticeship in the modern sector	1.4	5.8	9.3	6.9	9.5	0.0	0.0
Apprenticeship in the traditional sector	90.4	93.0	88.9	89.7	76.2	86.7	100.0
Family training	0.0	0.0	0.0	0.0	9.5	6.7	0.0
Total	100.0	100.0	100.0	100.0	100.0	100.0	100.0
Number of cases	73	86	54	29	21	15	17

SOURCE Arye (22)

than among the older generations (see Table 15). The numbers of people having undergone vocational training in an institution has not occurred at the expense of apprenticeship in the traditional sector but at the expense of apprenticeship in the modern sector. We would simply observe that the educational level of employers who had themselves been apprentices in the traditional sector is considerably lower than that of former apprentices in the modern sector and of those who have undergone proper vocational training. This confirms, as we have already seen, that the educational requirements for becoming an apprentice in the traditional sector are minimal compared with the demands of other systems: apprenticeship in the modern sector, the institutionalized education system, etc.

The duration of apprenticeship varies very greatly (from 1-2 years up to 12-16 years), not only from one country to another, from one activity to the next, but also from one enterprise to another.[1] There is no survey which enables one to study the length of apprenticeship according to the educational level of the apprentice and to test whether an increase in the basic level allows a reduction in the length of the apprenticeship. However, there are many indications that this link is weak. In fact it appears that if apprenticeship plays an important role in the training for a job and the transmission of knowledge, it performs many other functions, such as furnishing very cheap labour.

Lastly, it should be noted that apprenticeship does not perform an identical role in all branches of the economy. While it does seem to be important in handicrafts, small-scale manufacturing and services (in Dakar: electrical repairers, brickmakers, furniture-makers, watch-repairmen; in Ouagadougou: artistic artisans, tailors, furniture-makers, small services; in Nouakchott: manufacturing and services), it is less prevalent in the building industry

---

1. In Abdijan it lasts 6 years on average for carpenters; for master tailors it varies between 2 and 12 years, averaging 4.3 years (for 70 per cent of entrepreneurs, however, training lasts between 2 and 16 years) (Lachaud (*41*)). In Ouagadougou (Van Dijk (*25*)), entrepreneurs' apprenticeships lasted 4.7 years on average, varying between 7.5 and 6.9 years on average for straw-weavers and artistic artisans to 2.8 in trade and 3.5 in clothing. In Kumasi the average duration is 3.5 years; 44.1 per cent of employers have undergone apprenticeships of at least 3 years, and 18.7 per cent over 5 years.

and trade. This is probably due to the way these sectors work. In trade, for example, it does not take very long to learn the business (the obvious example of this is street peddling), but it is also likely that businessmen, having no need of plentiful labour, prefer, where necessary, to make use of family labour. The situation is more complex in the building industry: for one thing the distinction between traditional and modern sectors is relatively blurred: contractors, having a very fluctuating demand for labour, hire unskilled labour for the duration of a project, or else sub-contract out a portion of the job to traditional-sector contractors, thereby permitting a perpetual to-and-fro of labour between the two sectors; further, there is no very clear distinction between apprentice and worker in this sector, and contractors employ workers only for the duration of a contract.

These last examples now bring us to a more detailed study of the career histories of entrepreneurs in the traditional sector.

F. Professional experience of small-scale entrepreneurs

Career history data on entrepreneurs are relatively scarce. It appears, however, that mobility is quite high between jobs in the traditional sector or between the traditional and modern sectors. In Nouakchott mobility varies between sectors of activity: in the construction sector, 64.8 per cent of heads of small firms are currently in their third job or more (43.2 per cent are in their fourth or more), which confirms the remarks made earlier about the job mobility of workers in the building industry; in services and manufacturing, on the other hand, 61 and 54 per cent respectively of entrepreneurs have had one or two jobs at most.

In his study on African artisans King (16) analyses the career histories of a number of artisans in the traditional sector in Kenya, showing their extreme mobility between jobs: apprentice in the traditional sector, worker in the same sector, employee in the modern sector, small tradesman, then return to the traditional sector. Before setting up definitively, an entrepreneur may have had up to fifteen different occupations. In the carpentry trade in Abidjan de Miras notes that after his apprenticeship, the worker may work an average of nine years for different industrial firms in his branch before establishing his own carpentry business.[1] However, this great mobility does not mean that employment in the traditional sector is purely a transitory stage before entering the modern sector. In fact, in Dakar, Ouagadougou and Tanzania one observes stays of rather long duration in the traditional sector: this may reflect the relative fragility of traditional enterprises and the continuing process of their creation and dissolution. Penouil observes that between some 10 and 20 per cent of the firms would be dissolved per year and at the same time a large number are created: 54.5 per cent of garages and 48.6 per cent of tailors' workshops are less than a year old in Abidjan.

It is particularly interesting to examine links with the modern sector, and especially the number of entrepreneurs who have held salaried employment at some time. In Dakar, 64.8 per cent of masons have had a salaried job before setting up on their own account, as have 52.7 per cent of carpenters; the figure for electrical repairers (36.1 per cent), mechanical repairers (35.2 per cent) and metalworkers (34.6 per cent) is far from negligible too. In these trades it would appear advisable to spend some time in the modern sector to gain professional experience and skill in certain techniques. Indeed, Van Dijk shows that those who have worked in the modern sector are generally more dynamic: their turnover is higher, as is their initial capital and their income. It is difficult to pinpoint the reasons for this: have they really learned something in the modern sector, or were they simply more dynamic by temperament, which would have enabled them to gain selection to this sector? Did they manage to save and accumulate a certain amount of capital by working in the modern sector? Or is it a bit of all these factors? It should be noted that 51 per cent of Dakar natives and 53 per cent of former migrants (resident more than twenty years in Dakar) have been employed in the modern sector, and that the proportion declines significantly in step with length of residence in the city, falling to 12 per cent for those who have only lived 5-10 years in Dakar. This shows that recent migrants have not yet had the time to find work in the modern sector. It also enables us to verify the hypothesis of a certain career pattern for migrants. Many of them arrive in Dakar and begin by spend-

---

1. Even so, the author specifies that it is not necessarily the worker's position as wage-earner that enables him to build up his initial capital.

ing some time unemployed, before finding work as an apprentice and/or worker in the traditional sector; they then go to work in the modern sector as unskilled labourers or skilled workers and, on reaching their ceiling in terms of income and rank in this sector (owing to their lack of qualifications, they cannot hope for any big promotion in the modern sector), and provided they have saved enough, they then return to the traditional sector in order to set up on their own account. This hypothesis is highly plausible in the case of Dakar, where entrepreneurs have been resident in the city for quite some time already and are no longer all that young.

In Nouakchott 51.9 per cent of small-scale entrepreneurs have worked in the modern sector before becoming employers themselves. The likelihood of passing through the modern sector is all the greater when the employer had had an institutionalized vocational training (83.3 per cent) or undergone an apprenticeship in the modern sector itself (72.7 per cent), but even among entrepreneurs having done their apprenticeship in the traditional sector, the proportion having worked some time in the modern sector is still fairly high: 51.3 per cent. In Tanzania, lastly, we find that the proportion of entrepreneurs having had a salaried job varies considerably depending on the job. It is very high among building contractors (73 per cent), which accurately reflects the very close links that exist between the modern and the traditional sectors in this industry. It is average among artisans and hotel and restaurant managers (respectively 45 and 52 per cent), although transfer from one sector to the other is relatively easy. In certain branches of activity, the self-employed continue to work in the modern sector; this is true for 37 per cent of estate managers and farmers. The linkage with the modern sector appears to be weak in the case of two occupations: street pedlars (39 per cent), who are often too young to have had an opportunity of having a salaried job; and shopkeepers (37 per cent), since this is generally a stable occupation.

From the point of view of the past experience of entrepreneurs and their links with the modern sector, we may attempt to outline a certain classification of jobs in the traditional sector, distinguishing between purely traditional handicrafts, occupations with a rather more modern content (after-sales service), where one more frequently comes across people having worked in the modern sector, and jobs in the building trade, where mobility between sectors is the rule. This classification requres testing in the light of working conditions and earnings.

G. Working conditions and earnings in the traditional sector

Before concluding this panorama of characteristics of workers in the traditional sector, it is worth taking a look at the specific working conditions prevailing in this sector. Most surveys analyse workers' earnings in detail, but they rarely concern themselves with the duration of work itself (see Appendix Tables 7 and 8).

1. Duration of work

One characteristic of the traditional sector is precisely its irregular working hours and low productivity. The survey of Tanzania reveals a far greater range of working hours than in salaried employment, either because workers tend to work less, because business is irregular or demand insufficient, or because they tend on the contrary to work longer hours than in the modern sector, their shop or workshop requiring long hours of presence waiting for customers to turn up. Thus, 28 per cent of street pedlars work less than five hours per day, but 22 per cent work more than eleven hours. In the artisan sector, 22 per cent work less than five hours a day, while only 7 per cent of salaried employees do so. In shops, 34 per cent work more than eleven hours a day, whereas only 7 per cent of wage-earners do so. In the building trade, what varies above all is the number of days worked per week. Owing to the irregularity of contracts, 22 per cent work three days or less per week.

In Dakar the number of hours worked is relatively high, probably higher than in the modern sector, for less output. Metalworkers and furniture makers for instance work 54 hours a week, and mechanical repairers work a 56-hour week.

These difficult working conditions have to be contrasted with the level of earnings.

2. Analysis of earnings of workers in the traditional sector

Earnings in the traditional sector are generally very inferior to those in the modern sector. A few figures will illustrate this statement: average earnings in the traditional sector are equivalent to only 35 per cent of modern sector earnings in Asunción, 39 per cent in San Salvador, and 52.3 per cent in Santo Domingo. Even if we exclude domestic service, the situation remains highly favourable to the modern sector, since average earnings in the traditional sector still amount to only 44, 53 and 54 per cent of earnings in the modern sector in Asunción, San Salvador and Santo Domingo respectively. Earnings curves taken from the PREALC study clearly illustrate the great inequalities of income between the domestic and non-domestic traditional sector, on the one hand, and the public and private modern sector on the other (see Figures 1, 2 and 3). In all three countries, it is in domestic service that wages are by far the lowest (between 94 and 96 per cent of domestic servants are paid below the minimum wage), followed by the non-domestic traditional sector, which pays low wages to most of its employees but does enable a few of them to earn high wages; lastly, the public sector and of course the private modern sector (where, with the exception of San Salvador, the earnings spectrum is far broader).

A household survey conducted in Tananarive (Madagascar) in 1968/69 [1] reveals similar earnings disparities: artisans, representing 10 per cent of the population, received only 7 per cent of monetary income and 7.4 per cent of total income. Similarly, small services and pedlars, representing 7 per cent of the population, earned only 1.5 per cent of monetary incomes and 1.2 per cent of total income. Monthly incomes in this sector were 7.5 times below the urban average.

It happens, however, that in certain countries and for certain activities, earnings in the traditional sector may be equal or superior, if not to average wages in the modern sector, at least to minimum wages in that sector. In Kabul (Afghanistan), for example, the income of an owner-manager of a shop or of a male worker in trade is higher than that of a skilled worker.[2] Just as unskilled young workers in the traditional sector earn a higher

---

1. INSEE, *Budgets ménagers urbains en 1968/69 à Tananarive*. Paris, 1971, cited by IEDES (7).
2. "Sectorial interdependence in urban labour markets and variations in their social and economic development", by James Scoville, in *Studies of urban labour market behaviour in developing areas*, edited by Subbiah Kannappan, IILS (42).

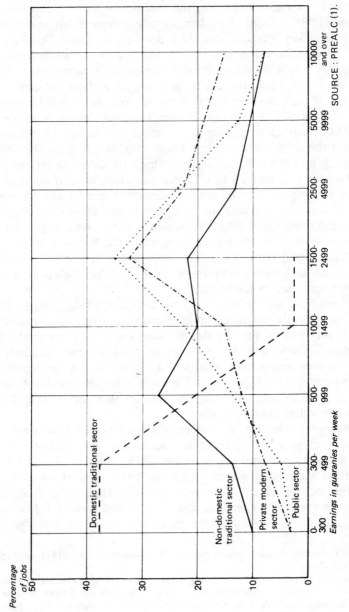

FIGURE 1. Asunción, job structure in terms of income scale, 1973.

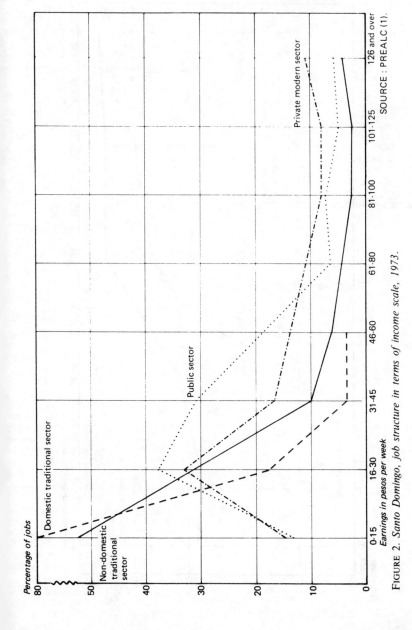

FIGURE 2. Santo Domingo, job structure in terms of income scale, 1973.

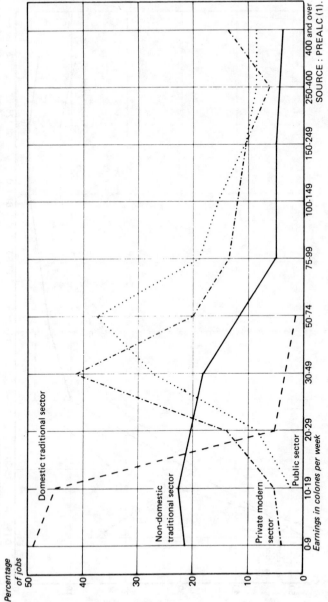

FIGURE 3. San Salvador, job structure in terms of income scale, 1973.

salary than that of an unskilled worker in the modern sector. In Nigeria, the situation varies from one state to the next (*43*): average earnings in the traditional sector are inferior to those of an unskilled worker in the public sector in the States of Kwara or Mid-Western, whereas in Lagos the average earning of workers in the traditional sector are equivalent or even higher. In Nouakchott the average income of an entrepreneur in the handicraft, construction and service sectors is distinctly higher than the minimum wage of a skilled worker in the modern sector. In Abidjan, in the clothing sector, the income of an entrepreneur is on average 25 per cent higher than the legal minimum wage (Lachaud (*41*)). In Dakar (Van Dijk (*24*)), the average income of the head of a firm in handicrafts, manufacturing and repairs is more than twice the average wage of a labourer in the modern sector.

The situation and income prospects therefore vary a great deal from one country to another. In many cases traditional sector incomes appear competitive with those of the modern sector, and for somebody whose qualifications are very low and whose prospects in the modern sector are accordingly limited, it may well seem a better bet to set up on one's own account. In reality though, things are not quite that simple: for the figures quoted above are averages, and give no indication as to income distribution. In developing sectors where demand is growing and supply as yet inadequate, small-scale entrepreneurs can generally hope for satisfactory earnings, somewhat superior to what they could hope to earn in the modern sector; some will even earn very high incomes, bearing in mind the very cheap labour they employ (unpaid or barely-paid apprentices and a handful of workers). In the sectors in recession or saturated, where demand is slack and restricted, but where competition is fierce, a few entrepreneurs will net big incomes, but the majority will just about make ends meet, even though they use cheap labour. It is therefore essential to analyse incomes separately, by occupational group and/or sector of activity, and to distinguish entrepreneurs from the labour they employ.

(a) *Earnings levels and sector of activity.* We may distinguish several groups of occupation within the traditional sector:
1. In certain occupational groups and sectors of activity earnings are very low.

In his study of migrations and occupational marginality in Mexico City Garcia Olivera Stern (44) distinguishes five main groups with incomes below the legal minimum: unskilled workers in the service sector (12.7 per cent of the working population, of whom 77.9 per cent earn less than the legal minimum wage); unskilled manufacturing workers and street pedlars (2 per cent of the working population, of whom 62.4 per cent earn less than the legal minimum wage); unskilled building labourers (1 per cent of the working population, of whom 64.9 per cent earn less than the legal minimum wage); and lastly farmers. This classification could also very well be applied to San Salvador, where almost all domestic servants, employees of other types of personal service, street pedlars and a fairly large proportion of artisans and manufacturers (64 per cent) earn less than the legal minimum. A survey on street pedlars and hawkers in South-East Asia (MacGee) shows that 50-70 per cent of them earn less than the legal minimum. In Nouakchott and Lomé, even in the traditional sector, called modernisable, some entrepreneurs in the service sector earn very low wages.[1]

We may thus distinguish an initial category of workers in the traditional sector (the most marginal), among whom we find chiefly domestic servants, street pedlars, small personal services (shoeshine boys, small repair shops, cobbler, etc., money changer, prostitutes), but also all those occasional workers, and a few small manufacturers or building contractors, as well as old workers who can no longer find work, the disguised jobless. All these people exercise a very wide range of (very irregular) activities, earning roughly the minimum needed to keep body and soul together.

2. In the second group of occupations, entrepreneurs earn a variable income that is often equal to or even slightly above that of

---

1. In Nouakchott the least-well paid entrepreneurs in the services sector (last decile) earn very low incomes, equal to a quarter of the wages of a salaried worker. In Lomé, this same category of entrepreneurs earns only a third of the wages of a skilled worker in carpentry, a fifth of the corresponding wage in the building trade and electrical repairs, and even one-tenth of the corresponding wage in the small mechanical repairs business.

a worker or clerk in the modern sector. These entrepreneurs are generally to be found either in traditional handicrafts or shopkeeping, building and some more modern service enterprises. The sectors offering the highest wages are not the same in every country. It depends on the extent of competitivity and on the firms' characteristics (size, etc.). Sometimes it will be in construction, commerce or repair services (activities which in other countries may already be overcrowded).[1]
3. In certain sectors some entrepreneurs are able to earn substantial incomes. This is mainly the case in the more modern sector: construction, after-sales services, electrical or mechani-

---

1. In the traditional sector in Asunción 48 per cent of industrial workers, 66 per cent of tradespeople, 44 per cent of workers in repairs, and 51 per cent of other service personnel earn more than the minimum wage; 33 per cent of shopkeepers earn over twice the minimum wage. In the building industry the average salary of a worker in the traditional sector is no more than 40 per cent of the salary of his counterpart in the modern sector, but the few workers with more than seven years of education earn close on double the earnings of their opposite number in the modern sector.

   In San Salvador 70 per cent of workers in the repairs sector and 47 per cent of tradespeople earn more than the minimum wage. Employees in repairs and other services and workers in the building trade in the traditional sector earn the same, or almost (90 per cent in the building trade) as their counterparts in the modern sector. In Santo Domingo incomes in the repairs services represent 72-77 per cent of earnings in the same activity in the modern sector.

   In Ouagadougou average earnings of entrepreneurs vary considerably from sector to sector, ranging from 1918 CFA Francs for straw-weavers to 17457 CFA Francs in the building trade. Those sectors in which incomes are below the average for all activities taken together tend to be those which, like traditional handicrafts, are "on the way down": straw-weavers, weavers, but also tailors and carriers, while the sectors where earnings are well above average are first trade, followed by construction.

   In Dakar, too, average earnings of entrepreneurs vary considerably according to their type of activity, although they are in all cases well above average labourers' earnings in the modern sector. The lowest average earnings are those of watch-repairmen, followed by electrical repairers, while earnings in excess of the average figure for all those interviewed are to be found in the building trade and in carpentry.

   In Nouakchott incomes are considerably higher in construction (9670 UM) than in the services (5220 UM) or in manufacturing (4939 UM). In the former sector even the incomes of the least-well paid entrepreneurs (1st decile) are well above those of skilled workers in the modern sector.

cal repairs, transport, trade in imported goods. Thus in Nouakchott one finds that the 10 per cent best-paid entrepreneurs earn close on ten times the earnings of modern sector employees in manufacturing and the services, and twenty-five times higher in the building trade. In Lomé the most dynamic entrepreneurs (last decile) earn close on six times (carpentry and metalwork, building) or seven times (electrical repairs) the earnings of a skilled worker in the modern sector.

The classification outlined above to a large extent complies with the division of the economy into a handful of main sectors (small personal services, traditional handicrafts, repairs, and the building industry), but it also cuts across branches of activity. Clearly, the branch is not an adequate criterion for classifying enterprises. For one thing, certain branches may be expanding in one country and saturated or declining in another. Also, several types of enterprise coexist inside a single branch. To clarify this typology we would need—as we suggested in Chapter I—other kinds of data concerning the activities and control of the modern sector, possibilities of link-up and sub-contracting with and for this sector, and the state of demand and competition within the traditional sector.

(b) *Analysis of incomes according to status of employment.* Incomes as high as those observed in certain African cities are only possible through the use of extremely cheap labour. Indeed, apprentices—and even workers—are barely paid at all. Sometimes the apprentices even have to pay for the right to become indentured. Thus in many of the manufacturing and services sectors in Abidjan apprentices are not paid—or rarely so. They are fed and housed by the master, who receives a fee from the apprentice's family. De Miras *(38)* concludes that "apart from one meal a day provided by the employer, either in kind or in cash, the cost of upkeep falls mainly on their family, which is what makes it possible for this subsistence sector to function and to produce a net surplus". In Ouagadougou not only do three-quarters of the apprentices receive nothing, but what is more there are very few who are fed, housed or clothed. In Dakar apprentices earn a certain wage, but one observes considerable variations from sector to sector: the lowest wages are to be found in the sectors which are easily accessible (watch-repair, electrical repairs), whereas in the construction sector, where the distinction between apprentices and workers is slight, wages are considerably higher.[1]

In Latin America apprenticeship is not as widespread as in Africa. Young people are very often hired as *ayudantes* (unskilled workers), both in the traditional and in the modern sectors, until they have learned their trade, and receive a very low wage close to or slightly below the minimum wage. Consequently earnings disparities between workers in the modern and traditional sectors are not very large, not as large at any rate as for other categories of workers.[2] This might explain why, in Latin America, entrepreneurs use far fewer apprentices than in African or Arab countries, but use family workers instead; this helps to produce slightly different ground rules and a slightly different composition in the traditional sector in Latin America from those prevailing in Africa. It would be interesting to have more detailed data on Latin America as well as similar information on Asia for the purpose of comparing the workings of the traditional sector in different contexts.

---

1. In Nouakchott apprentices earn a quarter of what a labourer in the modern sector earns. Although incomes vary little between sectors, they are lowest in the services.

    In Dakar apprentices earn on average 833 CFA Francs per week, but there are considerable differences between the sectors, from 225 CFA Francs on average for apprentice watch-repairmen, to 1406 CFA Francs for masons. In general, incomes are very low in the sectors that are easiest to enter: watch-repair, electrical repairs; average in the other sectors; and relatively high in the building industry, where the distinction between apprentice and worker is very weak. It should be noted that the very great majority (93 per cent) are fed, but that relatively few are housed.

    In Ouagadougou, 74.6 per cent of apprentices receive nothing, 11.6 per cent are housed, 27 per cent are fed, and 12.3 per cent are clothed. Those that are paid receive on average 631 CFA Francs per week; this varies considerably according to sector. In general one comes across the worst-treated apprentices (inasmuch as more than 80 per cent of them receive nothing at all) both in the relatively modern sectors (construction, trade) and in the highly traditional ones (straw-weaving, weaving).
2. In Asunción, for example, traditional sector wages as a percentage of those in the modern sector are 64 for workers, 42 for office workers, and 25 for employers. In San Salvador, the percentages are 69 for workers, 35 for office workers, and 40 for employers.

III. Education, training and access to the traditional sector

After making a few contributions towards an answer to the question "Who is in the traditional sector?" and showing, in particular, the extreme diversity of profiles in view of the great variety of occupational categories belonging to the traditional sector, we now move on to the more general question of the relationship between the education system and the traditional sector. This relationship can be analyzed by means of two questions:
— Is there a macrostatistical relationship between the development of the education system and the development of the traditional sector?
— Do education and/or training play a role in maintaining and developing the activities of the traditional sector?

A. Development of the education system and the traditional sector

The initial work carried out on the relationship between education and economic growth, by Stroumilime and then Denison, established education's contribution to economic growth by making use of econometric models which regard education as a residual factor of growth (cf. (12)). These works led to the conclusion that education promotes growth, and showed that a large proportion of growth (23 per cent according to Denison) could be explained by educational development. However, these studies are over-general and do not distinguish economic activities according to whether they are of a traditional or modern nature, and they analyze the evolution of "mean value added" without any breakdown by sectors. It is accordingly impossible to deduce any information concerning the role of education in development of the traditional sector. Moreover, an answer to this question would imply the existence of a theory connecting educational deveopment and growth strategy, permitting thorough examination of the following two queries: What type of education? For what growth strategy? Unfotunately, we have neither such a theory nor systematic empirical data permitting suggestions to be made towards an answer to these questions.

At best, and indirectly, we can find in specialized research on the traditional sector information concerning the contribution of basic education to the increase in labour *supply* in the traditional sector by means of migration, and assess the existence of a parallel between the level of educational training development and the development of the traditional sector.

1. Education, migration and labour supply in the traditional sector

Several writers have denounced, over the last ten years, the active role played by education as a factor in the rural exodus and the swelling of the labour reserve in search of work in urban areas. The main arguments are that: (i) education is ill-adapted to the requirements of people living in rural areas; (ii) education encourages migration towards the towns by informing the rural populations of the much higher living conditions prevailing in urban areas; (iii) education curricula have been designed with reference to a system of values giving priority to the city; (iv) further studies following completion of the compulsory-schooling period generally require emigration towards the city.

While one can hardly place on education alone the responsibility for the rural exodus, whereas everyone agrees (*31*) that it can be explained by the great difference between income and living-standard conditions between the city and the country, one must nevertheless admit that education plays at least a "supporting" role among the factors leading to migration. Table 16, taken from the critical study on the causes of rural migrations by J. Gaude (*32*) shows, by means of a comparison of the results of a few empirical studies, that education is rarely the chief determining factor in migration (Venezuela), but frequently represents the "second" factor explaining this migration (West Nigeria, Mexico,

TABLE 16. Specifications and principal determinants of some migration functions.[1]

Country	Type[2]	Specification[3]	Statistical unit[4]	Principal determinant[5]	Secondary determinant[5]	$R^{2\,b}$	Df[6]	Sources
Kenya (1968 survey)	r.u.	LL	Rate	Men: income differential	Distance	0.78	293	Rempel (1), p.109
				Women: proportion of skilled urban jobs	Distance	0.81	293	
Kenya (1968 survey)	r.u.	LL	Men aged 15 to 50 already resident in town for 4 or more years. Flow	Urban income	Rural income	0.61	32	Huntington (1974)
Zambia (1969 census)	c.s.	L	Proportion of population emigrating between 1963 and 1969. Rate	Index of rural income	Education	0.80	22	Bates (1974), p. 549
West Nigeria (1971-72 survey)	r.u.	LL	Proportion of migrants in each family. Rate	Average age of rural family	Education	0.80	475	Essang (1974), p.17
Ghana (1960 census)	c.s.	LL	Men aged 15 to 54. Rate	(a) Men aged 15 to 54: income	Distance	0.91	32	Beals (1967), pp. 434 ff.
				(b) Men aged 15 to 24: idem	Idem			
				(c) Women aged 15 to 54: idem	Idem			
Tanzania (1971 survey)	r.u.	L	Men born in the country who came to town after age	Index of probability of finding an urban job	Average urban population	0.55	102	Barnum and Sabot (quoted by Yap, 1975), p. 60

Egypt (1960 census)	r.u.	LL	Men born in i and recorded at j in 1960. Flow	Size of origin population	Distance	0.75	172	Greenwood (1969), p. 286
Venezuela (1961 census)	c.s.	LL	Men who have been resident in town for less than one year. Flow	(a) Age 15-24: urban education	Distance	0.61	368	Levy and Wadycki (1972)
				(b) Age 25-54: distance		0.60	368	
Venezuela [b]	c.s.	LL	Males aged 7 and over as a proportion of the equivalent origin population. Rate	(a) No education. Degree of urbanisation in the destination region	Distance	0.79	368	Levy and Wadycki (1974), p. 383
				(b) Primary education. Idem	Distance	0.85	368	
				(c) Secondary education. Income in the destination region	Distance	0.87	368	
Mexico (1960 census)	c.s.	LL	Rate	Distance	Relative illiteracy	0.30	—	Ovedovitz (1974), p. 68
Brazil [c] (1950 census)	c.s.	LL	Flow	Age 15-29: income growth rate in the origin region	Distance	0.52	327	Sahota (1968), pp. 230 ff.
				Age 30-59: idem	Idem	0.571	327	
Colombia (1951-1964 census)	c.s.	L	Net migration rate in one region	Low rural income (especially amongst the young)	Population pressure and insecurity	0.40	124	Schultz (1971)
Jamaica [d] (1960 census)	c.s.	LL	Rate	Distance	Relative income	0.52		Ovedovitz (1974), p. 68

TABLE 16. (*continued*)

Country	Type[2]	Specification[3]	Statistical unit[4]	Principal determinant[5]	Secondary determinant[5]	R^2[6]	Df[6]	Sources
Dominican Republic (1960 census)	r.u. and c.s.	L	Wage- or salary-earning household heads recorded as emigrants living in urban or rural group in any province. Rate	Urban in-migration Regional wage differential Rural out-migration poor explanation	Unemployment rate	.726	20	Carjaval and Geithman (1976)
Costa Rica (1963 census)	c.s.	L	Census household heads classified as employees and recorded as in-emigrants in any city or town in any Canton. Rate	Regional wage differential	Average education	.527	20	Carjaval and Geithman (1974)
India (1961 census)	c.s.	LL	Men who have been resident in town for less than one year. Flow	Distance	Origin population	0.70	231	Greenwood (1971)
Philippines[e] (1965 census)	r.u.	LL	Rate	Men: distance (local migration) Women: idem	Average income in origin region Idem	0.78 0.70	89 89	Wéry (1974), p. 111
Indonesia	r.u.	LL	Rate	Rural unemployment	Education and age	0.74	1737	Temple (1974), p.188

Education, training and access to the traditional sector

| (1955-1972 census) Cross-section on 29 developing countries | r.u. | L | Differences between the urban rate of growth and the demographic rate of growth | Proxy for the size of the urban informal sector | Rural-urban income differentials | .42 | 25 | Annable (1972, p. 409, equat. 1a) |

1. It is a pity that the authors do not publish the partial results of the regressions: by entering the variables one after the other one is better informed about the degree of explanation of each one of them according to the order in which they are chosen to appear in the regression. In addition, one obtains valuable indications about possible multi-collinearity.
2. Type of sample: c.s.: cross-section analysis of states or provinces; r.u.: rural-urban migration.
3. Specification of the migration function: LL: Log Linear; L: Linear (since the dimension of the parameters is not independent of the units of measurement of the explanatory variables, in this case I shall only give the two most significant variables).
4. Flow: net volume of migration between two regions over one period; rate: flow divided by the population of the origin region; speed: rate divided by the population of the destination region.
5. Principal determinant: maximum value of the significant parameter in absolute value; secondary determinant: the most significant parameter. If two (or more) parameters have the same degree of significance, I have taken the one which is highest and has the expected sign.
6. R^2: Coefficient of determination; Df: degrees of freedom (number of observations less the number of coefficients to be estimated).
   a. Mertaugh (1976) uses the same type of dependent variable as Schultz (1971) for Colombia and Bates (1974) for Zambia. The migration rate used does not differentiate between migrants' origin and destination regions but measures the flow of net migration towards (+) or from (−) a region over one period in relation to the population of this region calculated at the middle of this period. See Mertaugh (op. cit., p. 70 ff.) for further details.
   b. The rate of unemployment in the origin region has the same intensity whatever the level of education, as does the rate of urbanisation in the destination region (op. cit., p. 371). Other results: the migrants' mobility tends to increase with education due to better access to information. Similarly, educated migrants seek out regions with large and diversified labour markets. See also Schultz (1975) who, using a different specification, on the whole confirms these results.
   c. Cf. also Ovedovitz (1974, p. 68) who, with a number of different explanatory variables, adds to the distance factor the degree of relative illiteracy, a result which also agrees with those established by Sahota, op. cit., p. 234.
   d. These results are confirmed in the main by Adams (1969).
   e. The migration equation was also calculated for the year 1960 and the results are similar to those for 1975.
   f. Here we are dealing with a time series over 17 years. The model is one of the few to use simultaneous equations where the rates of migration and the rural and urban wage rates are endogenous. The results given here are taken from the reduced form and deduced from the author's main conclusions.

SOURCE   J. Gaude, *Causes and repercussions of rural migration in developing countries: a critical analysis*. (World Employment Programme Research, Working Papers.) Geneva, International Labour Office, October 1976.

Costa Rica, Indonesia). Brigg (*33*), analyzing the factors involved in rural-urban migration in several developing countries, concludes with a typology which assigns a moderate but significant role to education as an explanation of migration (Table 17). However, to the extent that very high rates of rural-urban migration have been observed over the last twenty years (Kingsley Davis shows that from 1960 to 1970, between 35 and 80 per cent of urban growth in Africa is due to migration (18.2 to 76.8 per cent in Asia; 11.2 to 58.1 per cent in Latin America)) (*34*), it may be considered that the net effect of education on the growth of the urban population in search of work is significant.

More particularly, with respect to the employment of migrants,

TABLE 17. Determinants of rural-urban migration.

Determinants	Intensity of the influence		
	Considerable	Moderate	Slight
1. *Economic reasons*			
1a Per capita real income differential	*		
1b Possibility of finding employment	*		
1c Removal costs	*		
1d Relative difference in incomes of skilled and unskilled workers			*
1e Minimum per capita income level		*	
1f Public services		*	
1g Housing			*
1h Educational secondary		*	
1i Primary		*	
2. *Distance*		*	
3. *Information*	*		
4. *Other*			
4a Family status			*
4b Relatives or friends in town		*	
4c Marriage			*
4d Recreational needs and urban services		*	
4e Physical security			*
4f Climate			*
4g Psycho-emotional reasons			*

SOURCE P. Brigg (*33*).

"most migrants are employed in the informal sector of the economy..."[1] writes N. Carynnyk-Sinclair following a comparative analysis of studies on migration in several countries (35). The previous chapter confirms this commentary by analyzing the profiles of the workers in the traditional sector and showing that a large fraction of these workers consists of migrants, even if the position varies depending on the city and the activity. Table 18 sets out additional data concerning certain cities in South-East Asia and two African capitals.

To sum up, one may conclude in general that education encourages migration from rural areas towards the cities, thereby contributing to development of the labour supply in urban areas; some

TABLE 18. Migrants employed in the traditional sector.

1. *Towns of South-east Asia*		
Percentage of pedlars who have been in town for three years or less	Kuala Lumpur	12.0
	Malacca	4.0
	Manila	11.0
	Bamgimo	22.0
	Jakarta	31.0
	Bandang	20.0
2. *Dakar, Senegal, 1977*		
In town five years or less, as percentage of total	Metalworkers	29.5
	Joiners	23.0
	Electrical repairs	38.3
	Mechanical repairs	17.0
	All traditional sector	26.1
3. *Ougadougou, Upper Volta, 1976*		
Migrants resident in town (numbers)	Less than five years	66
	Five-ten years	63
	Total	300

SOURCE   1: (27);   2: (24);   3: (25)

1. PREALC (*1*) presents estimates of the "informal" sector's share of urban employment: Cordoba (Argentina), 37.6 per cent; Bogota (Colombia), 43.4 per cent; San Salvador (El Salvador), 46 per cent; Mexico, Guadalajara and Monterrey (Mexico), 41.5 per cent; Asunción (Paraguay), 57 per cent; Santo Domingo (Dominican Republic), 55 per cent; and the urban centres of Chile (39.9 per cent); Ecuador (45.4 per cent); Peru (33.1 per cent); and Venezuela (44 per cent). Cf. page 298.

specially dynamic job candidates of rural origin manage to find jobs in the modern sector, thereby contributing to expulsion from this sector of the less well educated or more demanding of the native city-dwellers. Several employers prefer to recruit migrants as unskilled labourers; other job candidates of rural origin make a large contribution to certain activities in the traditional sector, no doubt because they are unable to find a job in the modern sector. In this way, education contributes directly and indirectly to development of the labour supply in the traditional sector.

TABLE 19. Relationship between education and employment in the traditonal sector.

	Percentage of self-employed workers; non-remunerated family workers (1)		School-attendance rates, primary and secondary (2)	
	Year	%	Year	%
Egypt	1975	48.5	1975	58.0
Libya	1973	28.0	1975	100.0
Tunisia	1975	32.0	1976	58.0
Argentina	1970	25.0	1970	75.0
Bolivia	1976	54.0	1976	66.0
Ecuador	1974	46.5	1975	73.0
El Salvador	1971	35.0	1970	55.0
El Salvador	1975	44.0	1976	65.0
Guatemala	1976	52.0	1970	37.0
Honduras	1974	54.0	1975	56.0
Mexico	1977	38.0	1976	80.0
Paraguay	1972	58.0	1973	67.0
Uruguay	1975	26.0	1974	79.0
Venezuela	1977	30.0	1976	73.0
Cyprus	1976	36.0	1976	65.0
Hong Kong	1976	14.0	1975	80.0
Indonesia	1971	65.0	1970	49.0
Iran	1972	61.0	1970	54.0
Korea	1977	53.0	1976	85.0
Philippines	1976	55.5	1975	87,0
Singapore	1977	16.0	1976	80.0
Syria	1976	45.0	1976	79.0
Thailand	1976	75.0	1976	62.0

SOURCE (1) I.L.O. Labour Statistics Yearbook, 1978.
(2) Unesco Statistical Yearbook, 1977.

2. Level of educational development and traditional sector

Data concerning value added in the traditional sector are rare and partial. It is accordingly not possible to compare over a sufficient number of countries the level of value added in the traditional sector with the level of education. For this reason, we have selected an indicator giving an approximate idea of the level of development of the traditional sector, namely, the percentage of "self-employed workers and non-remunerated family workers" in the active working population, and an indicator giving an approximate idea of educational development, namely, the apparent rate of school attendance at the primary and secondary levels. The results, set out in Table 19, show that in spite of the negative value of the regression coefficient between the two variables ($m = -0.5$), the following generally accepted assertion does not appear fully justified: "As a country becomes more developed (according to the criterion of *per-capita* GDP), school attendance rates rise, and the role played by the traditional sector in its economy declines". Some data in the table tend, on the contrary, to confirm that development of the traditional sector may be stimulated by a rising level of education, in spite of the approximate nature of the indicators adopted. For example, between 1970 and 1975 the rate of school attendance in El Salvador increased from 55 to 65 per cent, while the percentage of workers in the traditional sector rose from 35 to 44 per cent. The low correlation coefficient arrived at (0.45) suggests, moreover, a more complex relationship between the two indicators adopted. For want of detailed information, the following section is devoted to apprenticeship, and shows its nature and the way in which this relationship should be studied.

B. Apprenticeship and the traditional sector

Apprenticeship is one of the means of providing long-term vocational training. The two main characteristics of these apprentices are: (i) They earn little; (ii) All daily attend either a vocational-training school, or a place of work where they more or less learn a trade. In reality, notes Claudine Bouquillon-Vaugelade, "this category is ambiguous, since apprenticeship conditions may vary greatly from one individual to another".

Firstly, there is the group of unemployed. "They are only there to avoid staying home doing nothing".

A second group, which is generally found employment by a relation, receives a certain amount of pocket money and may be fed by the master at midday, though seldom in the evening; the apprentice more or less learns a trade.

A third group is distributed among the various vocational schools: schools of police, horticulture, agriculture, the arts, and centres of industrial qualification; they are accordingly destined to work in the modern sector.

This section deals exclusively with the first two groups of apprentices, and especially the second, which may be characterized by the existence of a contract between the apprentice, or his legal guardian, and the employer; the apprentice works for the employer in return for a wage which usually increases during his apprenticeship, and the employer provides theoretical and practical training which may lead to awarding the title of "master craftsman", "skilled worker", or "artisan". As this pattern is far more usual in Africa than on the other continents, and in view of data available, the following reflections will be based chiefly on the African situation.

Apprenticeship activities are so important in the traditional sector that certain writers do not hesitate to characterize the employment structure in this sector by the low number of wage-earners and the disproportionately high number of apprentices.

Comparison with the modern sector strikingly shows the difference in labour structures, and in particular the role of wage-earners and apprentices in the two sectors. For example, Table 20 compares the case of small garages and large garages in Abidjan in 1973.

TABLE 20. Abidjan: workers and apprentices in garages, 1973.

	Small garages	Large garages
Workers	591	2186
Apprentices	1846	50
Number of garages	301	45

SOURCE (13)

TABLE 21. Percentage of apprentices in the activities of the traditional sector.

	%
1. In the artisan sector, Upper Volta, in 1970: large towns	45.6
country as a whole	40.0
In the small garages of Abidjan in 1973	53.4
At Ouagadougou in 1970	50.0
2. With the tailors at Abidjan in 1976	60.9
3. With a Tunisian cabinet maker in 1977 (6 apprentices, 1 worker, 1 artisan)	75.0
4. At Nouakchott in 1977: in the production sector	41.6
in the services	63.5
in construction	3.7
total	32.6
5. At Bamako in 1978: in the production sector	64.9
in the services	67.5
in construction	27.5
total	58.0
6. In ex-Western Cameroon with the artisans: production	26.5

SOURCE 1: (7); 2: (26); 3: (18); 4: (14), (36); 5: (14), (36); 6: (37).

Nihan (11), Van Dijk (25), Charmes (18) and many other researchers have shown the high number of apprentices among the workers in this sector (Table 21).

Unfortunately such statistics are rare, since the limits of "apprenticeship" are poorly defined, and several writers have mistaken "apprentices" for "unpaid family workers", owing to the large proportion of apprentices related to their employer by kin.

However, assuming that the data in Table 21 give significant indications as to the role of apprenticeship in the traditional sector, the question which comes to mind is: Why are there so many apprentices in the traditional sector?

An answer to this question would help explain the operation of the production units in this sector, and show the effects of apprenticeship on its development. There are several rival theories concerning this question, and we can simply illustrate the debate by outlining a few studies:

1. The best illustration of the thesis in favour of apprenticeship in the traditional sector is no doubt provided by G. Nihan's study of the "non-structured" sector of the city of Nouakchott (*11*). This study, based on the results of a random survey carried out in 1977, covers the activities in the so called "non-structured modern" sector, namely, woodwork, light- and heavy-metal work, mechanical and electrical repairs, motor-vehicle repairs, and construction.

In examining the number of apprentices in training in each sector of activity, the author observes that (i) the number of these apprentices is very high in the production sector and services, low (3.7 per cent) in construction, no doubt due to the fact that this sector "is at a stage of development closer than the others to the modern sector"; (ii) most of the apprentices are taken on by entrepreneurs who themselves acquired the qualifications required for their job only by apprentice training, which would tend to prove the effectiveness of apprenticeship in developing self-employed activities in the traditional sector (see, for example, Table 22); and (iii), the entrepreneurs devote up to 10 per cent of their work time to apprenticeship, which inclines one to reject the hypothesis of "an apprenticeship system of no value whatsoever in the firms of Nouakchott".

Comparing the various training systems, the author observes that those who have acquired training "in the non-structured sector have generally used this training as much as those who acquired their qualifications by apprenticeship in the modern sector or as students in a training centre", and concludes that "(a) training in the non-structured sector appears to be as productive as any other form of training in terms of retention in the occupation acquired (and apparently even far more productive for the services than apprenticeship in the modern sector); (b) nor does it appear to penalize the student concerned more than the other modes of acquisition of qualifications...", since in spite of the specific nature of the training, 51.3 per cent of the apprentices have not remained confined to the narrow sphere of the qualification acquired, and have held jobs in the modern sector, both public and private.

Completing his analysis by a comparison of the performances of different training systems, making use of four indicators (see Table 23), the author admits that "for three of the four vari-

TABLE 22. Nouakchott: distribution of the type of post-school training received by entrepreneurs: relative frequency compared with N (percentage), 1977.

Type of training	Sector			Total
	Production	Services	Construction	
Apprenticeship in the non-structured sector	64.3	84.2	21.6	58.0
Apprenticeship in the modern sector	23.2	5.3	48.6	25.2
Training in a vocational-training institute	1.8	5.3	8.2	4.6
No training	10.7	5.2	21.6	12.2
Total	100.0	100.0	100.0	100.0
Number	56	38	37	131

NOTE Notice the divergence of the results for the construction sector as compared with the other sectors. Almost 50% of the entrepreneurs in this sector acquired their qualification as apprentices in the modern sector. This is the first factor to be taken into account with a view to justifying the hypothesis that the construction sector is already undergoing the transition to the modern sector. Source: (*11*).

ables taken into consideration—profits, value added and work productivity—the artisans trained in the traditional sector attain results far inferior to those of the artisans trained otherwise"; "however"—he notes—"at the level of the utilization of capital input, the entrepreneur who has served his apprenticeship in the non-structured sector obtains far better results (*sic*) than those obtained by his colleagues...". This would be explained by the fact "that the productivity of fixed assets is higher for those firms with the lowest capitalization level". And this is the case of the traditional sector, which explains, according to Nihan, the poor performances of the entrepreneurs in this sector, since "the entrepreneur's profits and the firm's value added are correlated to the level of the firm's capitalization" (*11*). Accordingly, it is not the entrepreneurs' managerial abilities which are to be questioned. The author's conclusion is that: "... the apprenticeship process in the non-structured sector is important on the quantitative level with respect to both the number of apprentices at present employed in the firms and the number of entrepreneurs surveyed who have received

TABLE 23. Entrepreneur's profits (excluding partners), value added and productivity ratios, classified by types of entrepreneurial training, calculated for a normal week's work, Nouakchott, 1977.

Type of training	Individual profit (UM)[1] (average)	Gross value added (UM) (average)	Productivity of capital (average)	Productivity of work (average)	Number of cases
Apprenticeship in the non-structured sector	4 030 *3 298* [2]	*6 421* *5 748*	0.072	1 459	74
Apprenticeship in the modern sector	8 289 *9 972*	17 373 *20 267*	0.041	2 517	33
Training in a vocational-training centre	14 460 *10 855*	26 358 *17 138*	0.045	3 214	6
No vocational training [3]	10 241 *12 081*	24 578 *23 675*	0.027	2 614	16
Total surveyed	6 375 *6 906*	12 402 *10 623*	0.042	2 138	129

1. 1 ouguiya (UM) amounted, at the time of the survey, to $ 0.0206. Average profits per category, in fact representing the entrepreneurs' revenues, are, respectively, in dollars and by type of training: $ 83, $ 171, $ 210. The minimum wage of the skilled worker in the modern sector is $ 30.
2. Figures in italic = typical divergence.
3. The profit of entrepreneurs without any vocational training is high in absolute value. By comparison with the volume of capitalization of the firms concerned, however, it represents a far lower return on capital than that of the other artisans.

SOURCE (*11*).

no other training than that of apprenticeship. On the qualitative level..., what is to be questioned is not so much the training of the artisans coming from the non-structured sector as the level of their firms' operation. ... These artisans are penalized, in particular, by a lack of resources for investment".

Some of the assertions made in this study were rejected long ago by several authors; this makes the Nouakchott survey interesting for the debate. Accordingly, the observation that 10 per cent of the entrepreneurs' work time was devoted to training apprentices poses the problem of the method of estimating the time-budget, and what entrepreneurs mean by training activity; according to another table in the study of Nouakchott, one observes that out of 70 firms employing apprentices, only 35 declare they provide training for these apprentices; in other words, for 50 per cent of the firms, the apprentices exist but not the apprenticeship. Moreover, the validity of the passing on of qualifications by apprenticeship has been questioned by several authors (as will be seen, for example, in the following paragraph), and while Nihan rightly notes that a high percentage of entrepreneurs were trained by apprenticeship in the traditional sector—which indicates that this type of training is definitely effective—on the other hand, one notes that 51 per cent of the apprentices will not become artisans and will have to look for employment (at what level? the study provides no details) in the modern sector, public and private. Lastly, if it is true that one cannot ignore the low level of capitalization as an explanation of the low level of profits and value added in the traditional sector, nor can one assert, as the report does, that the entrepreneurs' managerial abilities are not to be questioned and that apprenticeship gives "performances" comparable with those of other, more organized training systems.

However, the key question one wonders about, and to which the report provides no answer, is: "Why does the traditional sector employ so many apprentices?" or "What is the role played by apprenticeship in enabling the firms in this sector to develop or survive?". If the author does not wish to give his opinion concerning the question as to whether the apprentices are employed as cheap labour, but on the other hand observes that "the apprentices are paid even when an opportunity cost is incurred by the firm due to their mere presence", one is all the more puzzled as to how to explain the behaviour of the entrepreneurs, who, we are to believe, recruit unskilled labourers, pay them, and provide them with training, thereby incurring an opportunity cost without receiving anything in return.

2. Another approach less favourable to apprenticeship and contributing towards a reply to the latter question, is illustrated by G. Arye's study of the town of Kumasi in Ghana (22). The study is a random survey covering a stratified sample of 298 production units in the artisan sector and the repair services located at Kumasi, Ghana (motor repairs and maintenance, blacksmiths, metal-workers, carpenters, tailors, wood sculptors, cane-weaving, shoes and leatherware). The sample covers exclusively male entrepreneurs.

Analysis of the breakdown of entrepreneurs by type of training confirms the results of the Nouakchott survey. 90 per cent of the entrepreneurs had been apprentices in the "informal sector", 5 per cent had been apprentices in the formal sector, and 3.4 per cent were trained in the public and private training centres. Moreover, noting that the "number of journeymen" and "number of apprentices" variables are closely correlated, Arye notes that the more apprentices a firm takes on, the more journeymen it hires to supervise them; accordingly, with Nihan, he concludes that "the training of apprentices is a concern of the entrepreneur".

Taking as his starting-point the observation that the income of entrepreneurs in the traditional sector with no formal education is usually lower than the income of their colleagues who have received training, the author wonders whether these income differences can be explained by education, or by other factors connected with the characteristics of the production establishment. The main hypothesis of the study is that education and training in the school system have a significant positive effect on the intensity of employment in the traditional sector. To support this hypothesis, Arye constructs a regression model connecting the "product" (dependent variable) with education, school training, apprenticeship, family origin, age, ethnic origin, previous jobs, duration of work, capital, number of journeymen and artisans, and the raw material (independent variables). A distinction is made between the direct and indirect effects of education on production.

Among the many results of the regression, the most relevant for this report is that the regression coefficients arrived at are (a) negative with respect to the number of apprentices per firm; (b) positive and significant for the entrepreneur's education and school training; and (c) positive and insignificant for the entrepreneur's training by apprenticeship in the traditional sector.

G. Arye explains the negative coefficient for the "number of apprentices" variable by the fact that the apprentices form a heterogeneous group consisting partly of non-remunerated family aids; by the fact that certain apprentices do not work *directly* in the production sector (gathering materials, errands, distribution of goods produced, etc.); and, by the fact that sometimes the master sends the apprentice out to his farm where he uses him as a farm hand! The apprentices accordingly serve as a labour force which can be "taxed and exploited at will", and the existence of apprentices does not necessarily mean the existence of apprenticeship, particularly since, as Arye remarks, the number of journeymen as compared with the number of apprentices is too small to permit satisfactory supervision for training.

Moreover, and correlated to this point, apprenticeship in the traditional sector is less effective than school education and training. The former system of training, according to the author, suffers from several disadvantages (22). For example, each entrepreneur has his own training rules, and "who can say what an apprentice should or should not learn?"; for the entrepreneur, the apprenticeship is above all a way of procuring cheap labour, and, the author concludes, "in its present form (this system) is incapable of providing the managerial and production training needed to meet the expansion requirements of the artisan sector".

In all, while they agree concerning certain points, the studies of Kumasi and Nouakchott lead to diametrically opposed conclusions with respect to the interest of and prospects for apprenticeship. In spite of the optimism of the Nouakchott report, it cannot explain why the entrepreneurs have such recourse to apprentices—if the latter are relatively well paid and receive an appreciable and significant training service. The Kumasi report pessimistically "explains" the recourse to apprentices by the fact that they form a cheap supply of labour for the entrepreneurs (in terms of both wages and time devoted to training); as, in any event, 90 per cent of the entrepreneurs in the traditional sector are ex-apprentices from the same sector, one might infer from this that apprenticeship, in spite of its defects and deficiencies, will remain in the future the best means of developing the activities of the traditional sector. Even if the author of the Kumasi study feels that school training results in better "performances", that "the best combination from the success viewpoint in the informal sector would appear to be middle-school education plus specific training in an institution", and even if he recommends policies of developing this method of preparation for employment in the

traditional sector, this does not mean that it is possible to develop the sector's activities by school education and training.
3. In fact, the two approaches outlined above do not aim at explaining the role of apprenticeship training in the development and maintenance of the traditional sector. While the first study provides a better knowledge of the firm's characteristics and the second study enables assessment of the contribution to production of various factors, with, for both studies, either implicitly or explicitly, a theoretical framework of the neoclassical type, limited in its application to the narrow bounds of the traditional sector without taking into account interactions with the other components of the production sphere, neither study really defines the role of apprenticeship as a working mechanism for the traditional firms, thereby enabling assessment of these firms' prospects for evolution. The more detailed approach (by trade monographs) employed by Charmes in Tunisia aims at meeting these requirements (*18*).

Analyzing the results of an interview with a cabinet-maker at Tunis, the author observes that in spite of the lack of skilled labour of which he complains, the artisan questioned retains his apprentices three years, before laying them off. This behaviour is due either to the fact that the apprentices' training is inadequate, or rather over-compartmentalized, since if the taking on of apprentices is to be profitable, they must be specialized in a small number of jobs; or it is due to the fact that skilled labour is hard to find when it is poorly paid.

Undoubtedly, the strong competition in the joinery sector is an incitement to compress costs and wages; however, the same competition, Charmes points out, should in theory be an incitement to raising the hourly wage; in reality, the theoretical competitive wage rate is beyond the operating possibilities of the small-scale sector, and the firms in the modern sector, which are able to pay wages at the competitive rate, have a fairly restricted capacity for providing jobs. Consequently, the labour market in the modern sector does not affect the labour market in the traditional sector (segmentation exists), and "the system evolves towards institutionalization of apprenticeship as a form of wage earning".

This is the beginning of the vicious circle "low wages,

increasing labour supply". In concrete terms, the lower the wage rate, the greater the supply of under-skilled labour (for apprenticeship); this leads to compressing the wage rate slightly more. The institution of apprenticeship as a form of wage labour means that the apprentices, at the end of their training period (third year) compete with the skilled workers and contribute to the definition of their wages; the less competent apprentices replace the unskilled workers, and the totally unskilled labourers vanish, to be replaced by beginner apprentices.

The systematic use of apprenticeship as a reducing-cost device accordingly explains the "rapid" turnover of apprentices, in spite of the lack of skilled labour. Apart from the fact that the remunerations paid to the apprentices are exempted from certain duties on wages, the apprentices can, after quick training, render the same services as a good worker; they need merely become specialized in specific tasks. Whereas the worker can perform all the manufacturing operations, each apprentice trained can only perform a single operation or a few.

One can accordingly understand the use made of this labour by the artisan. After hiring apprentices and workers over four years (see Table 24), the artisan attains normal operating conditions, with six apprentices and one worker, which enables him to make an annual renewal: two apprentices are laid off and replaced by two beginners. In spite of the Tunisian law of 2 March 1961 stipulating that the number of apprentices in joinery or cabinet-making may not exceed 30 per cent of the number of skilled workers (percentage raised to 40 in the construction sector in 1972), the artisan justifies himself by putting forward his main function as that of training the young (in the traditional spirit of the artisan sector).

In this respect, Charmes points out that in terms of remuneration (18), "six apprentices cost half as much as a skilled worker, and one may estimate that they perform at least the equivalent work to that of two good workers; this means a division of wage costs by four". Certainly, one is unjustified in extending this remark to the whole of the artisan sector, but in the spirit of this observation one can deduce certain consequences concerning the role of apprenticeship in the prospects for evolution of the traditional sector.

TABLE 24. Tunis: use of manpower in a joiner's workshop (installation December 1972; survey January 1977).

1973	1974	1975	1976
1 or 2 workers	1 or 2 workers	2 workers	1 worker
2 apprentices, year 1	2 apprentices, year 2	2 apprentices, year 3	
2 apprentices, year 1	2 apprentices, year 2	2 apprentices, year 3	
2 apprentices, year 1	2 apprentices, year 2	2 apprentices, year 3	
	2 apprentices, year 1	2 apprentices, year 2	2 apprentices, year 3
		2 apprentices, year 1	2 apprentices, year 2
			2 apprentices, year 1
1 or 2 workers	1 or 2 workers	2 workers	1 worker
6 apprentices	8 apprentices	10 apprentices	6 apprentices

SOURCE Charmes (*18*)

According to the theoretical framework for analysis of urban employment in Senegal applied by Olivier Lebrun and Chris Gerry (*13*), Charmes distinguishes between two possible patterns of evolution for the traditional sector:

(*a*) Sectors in which exists a classic situation of competition, whose development is determined by internal factors (such as the wood and mechanical sectors), and which are characterized by the domination of small production units (both in the number of units and the jobs provided). The wood sector has expanded massively, "pulled along" by the building construction sector; this expansion has resulted in tension on the labour market, with wage rises compensated for by price rises. The industrial sub-sector played no role in the appearance of these tensions, and aligned its prices on the price level practised by the traditional sub-sector. However, prices were unable to keep following wages when skilled labour became rare. Accordingly, the small workshops institutionalized apprenticeship in the hope of reducing wage tensions. In fact, this was not the case, since many small production units were set up employing almost exclusively apprentices, owing to the highly favourable production prospects in the branch; the phenomenon in question was due either to the intrusion of small capitalists from outside the branch by association with workers in the traditional artisan sector, or quite simply to a rapid transition in three stages from apprentice to apprentice-entrepreneur, and then entrepreneur, facilitated by the fact that these apprentices were able to retain a salaried job while at the same time developing their own workshops. Accordingly, in the wood sector, where "supply is constantly striving to catch up with demand", apprenticeship fulfils a twofold role: (i) contributing to the rapid training of highly specialized labour in special jobs liable, however, to produce apprentice-entrepreneurs working "on order" and "undeclared"; (ii) enabling head artisans to limit their wage costs by purchasing only the strict amount of work they require, which is made possible by the fact that the work force is highly divisible;

(b) Traditional sectors in decline, suffering the full backlash of the competition of modern industry (such as the leather and textile sectors), characterized by the predominance of small production units and industrial jobs. In the textile sector, the production techniques vary depending on the firm's size, mechanization being really encountered only outside of the artisan sector. As a consequence, whereas modern industry is characterized by high productivity rates, relatively high wages and moderate prices, the artisan sector has low productivity, low wages and uncompetitive prices. Accordingly, to enable it to survive, it tends to institutionalize apprenticeship as providing a cheap pool of labour, by seeing to a high rate of apprentice turnover and extending the apprenticeship period so as to reduce the cost of training. As competition with industry is strong and the supply exceeds the demand for the products of the artisan sector, positions are rare and costly; this induces the lucky ones who manage to find work on completing their apprenticeship, to accept low wages. As for the others, the majority, they set up their own business, competing in their turn with their ex-employer artisans. In Charmes' own words, "to face up to the competition of the strongest, capitalist industry, to preserve itself, then, the artisan sector forged the weapon of its own destruction, the competition of the weakest, the informal sector in the strict sense of the term."

All in all, one cannot answer the question: "What is the role of apprenticeship in the generation, development and prospects of the activities of the traditional sector?", without first posing the question as to the context within which the various branches of activity in this sector evolve: (i) Some are in decline and suffering the full backlash of competition from their counterparts in the modern sector, and the institutionalization of apprenticeship, which in theory enables (owing to low wages) the artisan sector and its sub-contractors to hold on, contains the seeds of their "destruction" in the long run. The generalization of apprenticeship without training will result in swelling the ranks of "marginal" workers and amateurs, who will compete "downstream" with the artisans, who will also have to face the "upstream" competition of the modern sector. This will result in lowered prices and constant degradation of the quality of the product offered for sale. It will also lead to a reaction by the modern sector, to supervise and control "entries" into the traditional sector, or request guarantees and protective measures;[1] (ii) Other branches are developing, owing to increasing market demand for the produce of the traditional sector. Price and cost inflation, here again, is leading to institutionalization of apprenticeship, with, as corollaries, the deterioration of workers' status and exploitation of young apprentices. As a consequence, depending on the case, apprentice training may either help accelerate the decline of the traditional sector, or contribute to its retention and development, usually by means of institutionalization of the artisan/apprentice system, which enables the former to make use of more or less specialized labour paid with disguised wages, and the latter to find jobs on a saturated market.

Without prejudging what will be said in the conclusion to this report, these observations show what is really at stake in the

1. A report for a meeting of the Ministerial Cabinet of Senegal in 1968 states: "Growing competition on foreign markets and competition with clandestine, illegal local production of soles (using self-employed piece workers to cut the rubber) has led BATA to request a re-examination of the protective agreement from which it benefits at present", quoted by Gerry, see (6).

debate which has been going on for some years concerning the merits of growth strategies assigning a larger role to the activities of the traditional sector, and concerning the consequences of the choice of such strategies for educational planning, and training by the formal system or by apprenticeship. It will be recalled that these strategies were chiefly designed to try and solve the problem of unemployment, which the growth strategy in vogue, based on large-scale indutrialization, has not managed to solve, and which one hopes to be able to solve by developing "labour-intensive" small-scale national industry.

Two lines of action have been followed since the beginning of the seventies (particularly since the publication of the report by the ILO mission on full employment in Kenya).

The first is to protect the "traditional artisans" from the competition of large-scale industry and clandestine entries into the profession by means of legislative steps (control and coding of access to these activities), fiscal and financial measures (all kinds of aids), and training and education measures ("to be an artisan you need such and such a certificate!", or "how to educate so as to produce self-employed workers?"). In reality, the examples in the monographs of Lebrun and Gerry on Dakar, Charmes on Tunis and De Miras on Abidjan appear to show that this option will lead to the disappearance of the artisan sector in the short or medium term, or in any case to the aggravation of employment problems in a relatively short period of time. In the first place, the formal training structures are inelastic in terms of supply, and inasmuch as access to the activities of the traditional sector is measured by the level of the formal-training "leavers", the growth of employment will be limited. Secondly, the control of apprenticeship and the brake placed on the growth of the artisan sector by regulations and the "subsidized" competition of small industry will lead either to the transition from artisan activities to small industry as a result of investments made by agents from outside the artisan sector and for the most dynamic artisans, by capitalization, or, and not exclusively, to the pure and simple disappearance of the artisan sector.

The second is to allow uncontrolled competition to grow up between artisans, small modern industrial entrepreneurs, and "clandestine entrepreneurs". This, as has been seen, enables labour-market tensions to be lessened, so that an ever-increasing number of migrants can survive in urban zones, and permits the development of economic relations (in particular, sub-contracting) between the various firms in the modern and traditional sectors. Paradoxically, this alternative is at once the most favourable and unfavourable from the employment viewpoint. It leads to the institutionalization of apprenticeship as a form of employment on low wages, and to the generalization of "disguised unemployment", or jobs paid at subsistence rates in the short and medium term. The institutionalization of apprenticeship, in the long term, sounds the knell of the artisan sector, since it subjects it to the competition of the modern sector and clandestine entrepreneurs.

Posed in these terms, the question creates a dilemma for economic and educational policy-makers. The future of the traditional sector will be either its transformation into small-scale industry, with few prospects of job creation, or its deterioration into a sector of activity employing increasingly underpaid and increasingly unskilled young labourers (apprentices). Should education play a role as part of a strategy for selection on entry to the traditional sector, or as an alibi for a policy which, under pretext of apprenticeship, simply permits subsistence by employing underpaid labour? These assertions and questions are simplistic and unqualified, and accordingly inadequate to faithfully describe a reality which is by nature complex. However, they have the merit of pointing out, by way of preface, as it were, to the conclusions of this report, the naivety of educational-policy slogans or proposals for education reforms such as: "Educate and train for traditional employment!" without evaluating the prospects for and contradictions in development of the traditional sector or appreciating the role played by education and training in this respect.

IV. The contribution of education/training to production in the traditional sector

For some years, concerned by the widening gap between the number of school-leavers and the job opportunities available in the modern wage earning sector, several aid agencies and various developing countries have advocated education policies to promote the traditional sector, pre-vocationalization of intermediate and secondary education, the diversification of secondary-education cycles, and the introduction of productive work into the primary- and secondary-education systems. As examples, we may mention the introduction of agriculture and technical and vocational subjects related to the artisan sector into the secondary schools in Pakistan, the pre-vocationalization of education curricula in Sri Lanka, secondary education for self-reliance in Tanzania, projects for the introduction of a basic 9-year education system, the last two years of which would be devoted to training for self-employment, in Kenya, projects to link up productive work and education in Zambia, etc. The objectives of these reforms are varied and numerous, but one of the major objectives is to encourage the pupils to become self-employed.

It may seem naive to try and work out education policies and plan reforms for development of the traditional sector when, as this document has shown, this sector can develop very rapidly, without any planned organization, simply owing to the pressure created by the arrival *en masse* of migrants to the cities and the inability of the labour market to provide jobs for all those who are looking for work, and when it is precisely those who have little or no education who are the first to enter the traditional sector. The cntradiction lies in trying to provide pre-vocational training for secondary pupils, already highly selected, with a view to encouraging them to enter the traditional sector, whereas precisely the fact that they belong to a select group, privileged both socially and educationally, will lead them to look for work in the modern sector, where work is more stable, better paid and less risky from numerous viewpoints. Some of these young people even prefer to remain unemployed for many months or even years rather than accept a job which seems to them unskilled. Probably, it is only when intermediate or secondary education has become generalized, in other words, when it will be as common to have a diploma from one of these education systems as it is at present to be literate, that one may hope to see these school-leavers enter the traditional sector in large numbers, whatever training curriculum they may have followed. The example of Ghana is very interesting in this respect. There, the level of education of entrepreneurs increases progressively as their age decreases, and this corresponds to the very rapid development of the school system. Some years ago primary and middle education were hardly developed. One finds, in fact, that no entrepreneur older than 60 has attended school, and that 73.7 per cent of those aged between 46 and 50 have likewise not attended school. Over the last ten to twenty years primary and middle education have developed very rapidly, and the proportions have been reversed; 16.3 per cent of those aged between 26 and 30 have received no education, and 68.6 per cent have attended middle school. The percentage of entrepreneurs who have undergone technical training, far from increasing, appears rather to have declined, from 6.7 for those aged 46 to 50, to 3.4 for those aged 36 to 40, and 2.3 for those aged 26 to 30. Whatever be their educational level, the very great majority still learns its trade "on the job" by working as an apprentice (93 per cent of those aged 26 to 30). Organized vocational training does not appear to have taken over, since it only affected 1.2 per cent of those aged 26 to 30 (as against 6.6 per cent of those aged 46 to 50).[1] In some ways the very rapid development of education has made possible a major rise in the

---

1. However, it is noted that the proportion increases, among those aged 20 to 25, to 6.8 per cent; is the trend being reversed? Apprenticeship on a wage-earning basis (modern firms) has, for its part, clearly diminished.

educational level of the workers in the traditional sector, but from one point of view the situation remains unchanged: apprenticeship remains the chief method for passing on knowledge and providing access to this sector.

The question is accordingly not what education should be provided to increase the informal system, but rather, should the traditional sector continue to develop in the same way as in the past, and should apprenticeship be allowed to retain a virtual monopoly of vocational training? What education must be developed for what traditional sector? How can education help improve the performances and productivity of the traditional sector?

What can we learn from existing studies on this question? There is very little research comparing variables of corporate development and entrepreneurs' income with the individual characteristics of the workers, in particular their level of education. Initial studies carried out in the sixties produced rather pessimistic results. A World Bank report on these studies notes:

> In a survey of Kenyan businessmen who had received the assistance of a State financial institution, Marris and Somerset discovered no correlation between the level of the entrepreneurs' education and their success. In a study on Nigerian shoemakers, Nafziger concluded that there was even a *negative* correlation between the education received by the entrepreneurs and the profitability of their firm. The author ascribes this fact to two causes. Firstly, the better-educated businessmen have not been able to acquire the practical knowledge required, and, secondly, in the past the more capable of these businessmen have preferred the higher-paid, more stable and more prestigious posts proposed to them by the civil service and foreign companies. For his part, Kilby observed, in his study on Nigerian bakeries, that there is a *neutral* relationship between the education received and business success. Harris, in his survey of Nigerian entrepreneurs, concluded that there exists "in practice, a significant correlation" between school education and success, but that this varies considerably from one industrial branch to another. He adds: "On examining each industry separately, one observes that education and success are positively correlated in the sawmilling, furniture, printing and clothing industries, that there is no correlation in the bakery industry and other similar activities, and that the correlation is negative in the rubber processing industry". However, in general, he found that the correlation between theoretical school education and the extent of the

entrepreneurs' success was "far less marked" than he had thought.[1]

These results may seem rather surprising. However, during the sixties, school-leavers were usually in high demand in the modern sector (administration, private and public enterprise), which constituted the logical opening for the very great majority of them. It is accordingly highly likely that those who entered the traditional sector were those who had not succeeded in the modern sector. With the advantage of initial privileges (probably coming from a high socio-economic milieu, with access to a large supply of capital), they did not, nevertheless, have the ability to succeed in the modern sector and preferred either to buy a small shop or workshop, or even set up a small firm in the traditional sector. This explains one of the conclusions of the World Bank report referred to above:

> Those with a higher level of education are usually driven by ambition and self-assurance to undertake ventures of a larger scale. If in many cases the results achieved by them are inferior to those of their less-educated fellows, this would appear to be chiefly due to their relative lack of technical knowledge, their tendency to launch major undertakings which they are unable to manage in practice, and their propensity for prestige expenditure.

More recent studies undertaken in the seventies lead to somewhat different results.

At Gran Asunción, Paraguay, average income increases significantly as the workers' educational level rises. At San Salvador, the same phenomenon is observed (see Table 25). However, it is interesting to note that the minimum educational level permitting a significant rise in income differs greatly depending on the branch of activity. In regular commerce, the basic services and

---

1. *The development of private enterprise in Africa* (2 volumes), Volume I prepared by John de Wilde, IBRD-IDA, December 1971.
Peter Marris and Anthony Somerset, *African businessmen: a study of entrepreneurship and development in Kenya,* Routledge and Kegan Paul, London 1971, p. 215.
E. Wayne Nafziger, "The relationship between education and entrepreneurship in Nigeria" *The Journal of developing areas,* Vol. 4, No. 3, April 1970.
Peter Kilby, *African enterprise: the Nigerian bread industry,* Hoover Institute Studies, 8, Stanford University, 1965, p. 92.
Harris, *Industrial entrepreneurship in Nigeria.*

The contribution of education/training to production in the traditional sector

TABLE 25. Income of workers in the informal sector, by sector of activity and level of education

	Gran Asunción, 1973 [1]	San Salvador, 1974 [2]					
		Industry	Construction	Regular commerce	Pedlars	Repair services	Other services	Domestic staff
0-3 years	980	39	35	31	25	38	36	10
4-6 years	1 396	30	35	44	26	39	64	12
7-9 years	2 389	32	47	46	28	100	154	20
10-12 years	4 798	69	ns	118	ns	73	156	18
13 years and more	1 745	ns	—	224	ns	—	278	—
Total		36	64	59	34	54	128	12

1. Guaranies per week. 2. Colons per week. n.s. = not significant.
SOURCE PREALC (1).

111

other private services, the fact of being "functionally literate" (over 3 years' education) brings about a major change in income, but the same is not the case for the other sectors. In the repair and construction services, the completion of primary education is a major advantage (as, moreover, for the other private services). In industry and regular commerce, those workers who have attained the level of the second cycle of secondary education have far higher incomes. In certain jobs, on the other hand, the level of education plays little role; this is the case for pedlars. The thresholds, or minimum educational levels, thus vary greatly depending on the type of activity. It is very interesting to note, secondly, that workers of the same educational level will have very different incomes depending on the sector of activity in which they are hired, and probably also depending on their job position (master, worker, office worker).

Paulo Souza and Victor Tokman have endeavoured to measure the respective effects of individual variables and structural variables on the income of workers as a whole, by means of various regression lines, based on the data relating to San Salvador and Santo Domingo. The first model introduces, firstly, the individual variables, measures the explained variance and endeavours to explain the remainder by structural variables.

(1) $Y = a + b_1 E + b_2 A + b_3 S + b_4 P + N_1$
(2) $N_1 = C + d_1 R + d_2 CO + d_3 T$

where:
E = education, A = age, S = sex, P = family situation, R = branch, CO = job position, T = size of establishment.

The second model introduces, firstly, the structural variables, and measures the amount of the remainder explained by the individual characteristics. These results are shown in Table 26.

In the first model, individual characteristics explain from 44 to 52 per cent of the income variance observed, and the education variable alone explains from 37 to 44 per cent of the variance (coefficient β^2 .137 to .195). This, however, concerns the incomes of all workers, in both the modern and traditional sectors. When we endeavour to cancel out the effects of the sector of activities and employment status (model 2) we notice that the role of education is greatly reduced. Indeed, once the effects of these factors are eliminated, the educational level explains only 3 per

TABLE 26. Income determinants at San Salvador and Santo Domingo (coefficient β^2)

	Santo Domingo		San Salvador	
	counting domestic staff	not counting domestic staff	counting domestic staff	not counting domestic staff
Incomes and personal characteristics:				
education	0.137	0.137	0.195	0.191
age	0.030	0.032	0.019	0.023
sex	0.037	0.033	0.020	0.017
family situation	0.008	0.009	0.009	0.007
R^2	0.462	0.448	0.525	0.503
Residual incomes and structural characteristics:				
branch of activity	0.002	0.002	0.010	0.011
position	0.031	0.030	0.053	0.051
size of establishment	0.022	0.021	0.024	0.019
R^2	0.251	0.247	0.277	0.230
Incomes and structural characteristics:				
branch of activity	0.025	0.012	0.034	0.023
position	0.024	0.024	0.111	0.114
size of establishment	0.047	0.049	0.053	0.058
R^2	0.361	0.340	0.395	0.354
Residual incomes and personal characteristics:				
education	0.001	0.001	0.114	0.044
age	0.028	0.029	0.016	0.020
sex	0.001	0.002	0.009	0.007
family situation	0.018	0.024	0.021	0.004
R^2	0.213	0.221	0.385	0.297

SOURCE PREALC (1).

cent of the residual variance at Santo Domingo or from 20.9 to 33.8 per cent of the residual variance at San Salvador, depending on whether domestic staff are included or not. These results clearly show that (i) the labour market is highly segmented, with major income differences between the modern and traditional sectors, both in general and for the same educational level; (ii) there is a marked correlation between the educational level and the employment sector and employment status: the more educated a person, the more likely he is to work in the modern sector, and to be an employer rather than a worker, etc.; (iii) at least at San Salvador, even when the effects of structural variables are eliminated, individual characteristics, and in particular the educational level, continue to play a major role in explaining income differences. It is not, however, possible by this analysis to isolate within the traditional sector the variables which are the most important in explaining income variations.

In his study of the traditional sector at Nouakchott, Nihan (*11*) compares certain indicators of entrepreneurial results in the traditional sector according to the type of vocational training followed by the entrepreneur. Table 23 (page 96) is highly significant; major differences are discovered in individual entrepreneurial profits, the firm's gross value added, and work productivity, depending on the entrepreneur's past record. The least successful are those who have undergone their apprenticeship in the non-structured sector, and those who appear to succeed best are those who have undergone training in a vocational-training centre. However, it should be pointed out that at the same time the fixed assets of the firms increase depending on the type of training received by the entrepreneur when he has undergone apprenticeship in the modern sector or followed vocational courses, and that the sound results of a firm may be explained by this fact. For example, it is observed that those entrepreneurs who have received no vocational training achieve results hardly inferior to the results obtained by those who have received formal training, but that they are also the ones who have managed, either owing to assistance from the family or their previous experience in the modern sector, to accumulate the largest amount of capital (their transition to the modern sector may have enabled them, moreover, to acquire the requisite qualifications). Without more sophisticated statistical analysis it is hard to evaluate the real factors affecting the firm's results; however, it is probable that if an entrepreneur passes through the modern sector and/or a vocational-training centre, he will acquire both the requisite qualifications and the means of accumulating the minimum capital required for his firm to succeed. This, however, remains to be tested.

At Lomé, Togo (*43*), the indicators of firm performance (individual profit and value added) increase significantly as the entrepren-

TABLE 27. Lomé, Togo: business performance indicators according to type of education of entrepreneur, 1978.

	Individual profit CFA.F		Gross value added CFA.F		Fixed assets CFA.F		Number of cases
	Average	σ	Average	σ	Average	σ	
Apprenticeship in the non-structured sector:							
no education	4 956	4 245	6 202	6 048	63 901	65 571	70
literate	6 870	6 538	8 222	8 038	159 442	358 784	52
incomplete primary education	7 534	7 650	9 186	10 141	164 226	287 703	62
complete primary education	9 652	8 711	12 892	12 335	278 188	544 686	74
secondary education	13 146	8 900	15 035	9 730	525 727	637 424	11
Apprenticeship in the modern sector	10 269	8 524	13 032	11 578	332 600	381 269	5
Training in a vocational-training centre	12 463	8 597	22 789	31 186	594 166	698 792	6
Total	7 701	7 409	9 830	10 822	194 796	400 405	280

SOURCE Nihan (43)

eur's educational level rises (see Table 27). The maximum levels are attained by entrepreneurs who have undergone secondary education plus apprenticeship in the traditional sector. Once the effect of the educational level is taken into account, the type of vocational training does not appear to play a decisive role; accordingly, the individual profit of an entrepreneur who has received training in a vocational centre after primary education does not differ greatly from that of an entrepreneur who has undergone apprenticeship in the non-structured sector after secondary education. Must we therefore conclude that it is the type of basic training which is the chief determinant of the results obtained? As in the previous study, the authors emphasize that the capital accumulated greatly increases as the entrepreneur's level of education rises, and that this latter factor is apparently most closely correlated to the firm's profit or value added. "The variations observed for the success indicators are no doubt due less to the entrepreneur's type of training than to a vector of economic factors in which the technological capital and intensity of capitalization probably play a significant role." Even if this is the case, however, the correlation between education and fixed assets seems sufficiently strong for one to be able to feel that education plays an effective role, whether directly or indirectly. This, however, was not measured in the study.

In his study of Kumasi (Ghana), Arye (22) measured the impact of the entrepreneur's educational level and type of vocational training on three indicators of firm performance: gross production, total profits and value added. He employed the following recursive model:

Capital $(Z_1) = f_1$ (educational level, age, racial origin,
$\qquad\qquad\qquad X_1 \qquad V_1 \quad V_2$
previous job, duration of work)
$\quad V_3\, V_4 \qquad\qquad V_5$

Job $(Z_2) = f_1$ $(Z_1$, educational level, age, racial origin, previous job, duration of work)

Raw material $(Z_3) = f_3(Z_1, Z_2, X_1, V_{j(1\to 5)})$

Dependent variable $(Z_4) = f_4(Z_1, Z_2, Z_3, X_1, V_{j(1\to 5)})$

In this way he was able to calculate the direct effect of the various individual characteristics, including education and vocational training, on the indicators of firm performance, the indirect effect of training in influencing the level of capitalization, the level of

TABLE 28. Kumasi: Direct effect of different variables on gross production: total gains in firm value added: regression coefficient (Z_4)

	Dependent variables		
Independent variables	Gross production (¢/week)	Total gains (¢/week)	Value added (¢/week)
Primary X_1	+14.40	+11.87	+12.90
Middle X_2	+34.06[2]	+31.88[2]	+33.00[2]
Technical	+26.34	+23.07	+23.37
Formal training	+94.37[2]	+95.02[2]	+96.14[2]
Training in the family	176.10[3]	174.86[3]	177.72[3]
Apprenticeship, traditional sector	39.64	42.14	41.60
Capital	0.01[1]	0.01[1]	0.01[1]
Raw materials	0.17[3]	0.17[3]	0.17[3]
Constant	48.30	55.37	45.84
R^2	73.2	12.8	14.5

1. Significant at the level of 10%.
2. Significant at the level of 5%.
3. Significant at the level of 1%.
SOURCE Arye (22). 1975 Survey.

employment and the amount of raw materials, and, finally, the total effect. Table 28 sums up the result of his regression analysis, and the most significant variables.

The most significant variables in explaining the production level and gross gains are the use of raw materials, taking into account the particular situation of chronic shortage which was prevalent at the time of the survey. Next come training in the family, training in a vocational-training centre, and the fact of having received middle-school education. Primary and technical education, although they have a positive effect on production, are not significant variables, and do not appear to permit as great an increase in production (as compared with no education at all) as middle-school education. This leads the author to conclude that primary education is inadequate to ensure complete literacy, which, on the other hand, would be provided by middle-school education. In the same way, compared with apprenticeship in the modern sector, apprenticeship in the traditional sector does not appear to have a significant effect or to make a major contribution to the rise in production. Only training in the family, and then training in a centre appear to play a significant role in increasing production.

Finally, one notes the positive but insignificant effects of the previous job held in the modern sector, the racial origin, and the relatively slight effect of capital, all other variables being constant, on production.

The indirect and overall effects confirm these initial conclusions. Moreover, primary education, technical education, racial origin and age have a positive and significant effect on capital accumulation, and their total effect becomes significant on production and value added. Table 29, summing up the direct and indirect effects, shows the primordial role of middle-school education and training in vocational centres. Apprenticeship in the traditional sector, which constitutes the principal means of access to this sector, does not play as positive a role as might be thought, taking into account, the author specifies, the very conditions in which the apprenticeship is performed (see previous chapter). Arye concludes by proposing as an optimum educational strategy for development of the traditional sector: (1) The generalization and improvement of middle-school education, where the entrepreneurs can become literate; (2) The organization of vocational training in

TABLE 29. Kumasi: regression coefficient of the direct and indirect effects of education on value added

Educational level	Direct		Indirect[1]		Total	
	Non-standardized	Standardized	Non-standardized	Standardized	Non-standardized	Standardized
Primary	—	—	5.46	0.0184	5.46	0.0184
Middle	33.00	0.158	—	—	33.00	0.158
Technical	—	—	9.34	0.0133	9.34	0.0133
Training in an institution	96.14	0.168	—	—	96.14	0.168
Apprenticeship in the informal sector	41.60[2]	0.120	—	—	41.60	0.120

1. Only the coefficients which are significant at least at level 0.1 have been used in calculating the indirect effects. Accordingly, the indirect effects due to the utilization of labour have not been included in the calculation.
2. Insignificant at level 0.1.
SOURCE Arye (22).

specialized centres, which should gradually replace apprenticeship.

These proposals, which are very attractive for the educational planner, deserve close study. It is likely that they are highly optimistic. In the first place, they are based on the fact that sound performances have been observed for the 10 entrepreneurs (out of a total of 298) who followed vocational training courses at training institutes. It is not impossible that their success is due to certain of their own characteristics, from the viewpoints of both their personal antecedents and their specific attitudes and behaviour. Moreover, it is hard to believe that training which has proved beneficial for 3 per cent of the sample can continue to be as beneficial when this training has been generalized for the population as a whole. It is probable that the operating conditions of both these training institutes (method of selecting students, training provided) and of the traditional sector, will change. Secondly, these training institutes are at present basically oriented towards the modern sector. Most of those who leave the institutes are destined for this sector or hope for a job in the sector. The institutes operate with curricula, facilities, conditions and a work atmosphere very remote from the requirements of the traditional sector. Costs are generally high. It is improbable that it will be possible to completely change these institutes' orientation. Lastly, as we have already seen, these proposals completely avoid the role of apprenticeship in the operation and maintenance of the traditional sector.

Other studies have endeavoured to measure the most important explanatory variables affecting the success of the small entrepreneur. For example, Van Dijk, exploiting data collected for his survey on Dakar, has adopted three success indicators: income, consumption level and level of employment of the firm. We shall mention, in particular, the results concerning income and consumption, which are indicators of the firm's sound management; only 38 to 47 per cent of the variance of these two indicators could be explained by the variables introduced in the model. The income level is explained by the initial investment, present investments, turnover, experience in the trade, technological level, experience in the modern sector, and the fact of keeping accounts, variables which have a positive impact on income. Consumption is explained by the level of initial and present investments, turnover, experience in the trade, age and work productivity, which are significant variables. Finally, the fact of keeping accounts is positively connected with the consumption level. None of the variables introduced in the model (or at least any significant variable) measures directly the influence of the entrepreneur's level of education. The only factors indirectly connected with his training record are the level of technology and the fact that he keeps accounts or not. From this data, it is hard to draw pertinent conclusions for the formulation of an educational policy in favour of the traditional sector.

The existing studies, as can be seen, do not provide a satisfactory reply to the questions posed above: What education for what traditional sector? The results do not always converge. However, it is possible to define a few points of agreement and draw some preliminary conclusions:

1. Firstly, at the present time, the relationships between the education system and the traditional sector are complex and dialectic. Although the education system does not provide training for the traditional sector, it is inaccurate to state that there is no relationship between them, since it is precisely the failures and rejects of the former which wind up in the latter. It is by its negative selection that the education system influences the profile of the traditional sector. Any proposal to develop education streams oriented towards the traditional sector must aim at a thorough overhaul of methods of student guidance and selection, criteria for selection of teachers, and training methods of the entire education system.
2. General education, above a certain basic threshold, permits a real increase in the entrepreneur's productivity. With respect to vocational training, the results of the studies are less conclusive. For Arye, institutionalized training gives better results than apprenticeship in the traditional sector; this also appears to be the finding at Nouakchott, while Nihan's study of Lomé shows that provided the entrepreneurs have a minimum level of education, the type of vocational training received is of little importance. It is probable that if one were to increase the number of studies of this kind, one would continue to find contradictory results depending on the sector of activity, the country, and the method of organization of apprenticeship or vocational training.

3. The educational requirements of the traditional sector vary greatly, depending on the sub-sector concerned (pure self-employed sector, disguised wage employment, or residual sector), the employment status, type of activity and size and level of development of the firm. A shopkeeper does not have the same needs as a building contractor or the head of a mechanical repairs workshop. An entrepreneur supervising two apprentices or employees does not require the same knowledge as a manager who already has a high turnover, more sophisticated machinery and ten or so employees. The former probably does not need to know much more than how to read, write and count, in addition to simple technical knowledge acquired during the course of an apprenticeship, whereas the latter must know how to win contracts, calculate and control costs, keep accounts, supervise product quality, plan his activities, obtain credit and manage skilled staff.
4. In spite of its deficiencies, apprenticeship is, and no doubt will remain, the chief means of access to the traditional sector in many countries. It is even probable, although the studies do not show this clearly, that the role of apprenticeship has increased over the last few years; whereas the old entrepreneurs were able to acquire their job qualifications in the modern sector, the young entrepreneurs have almost all served their apprenticeship in the traditional sector. This is due to the very dynamics of this sector's development; to face the competition from newcomers to the market or the modern sector, and so as to limit wage costs, the entrepreneurs are making increasing use of apprentices, who form a low-paid or unpaid source of labour. On the other hand, the unemployed accept this situation in order to find a job on a saturated market and have a chance of subsequently setting up on their own. The quality of the apprenticeship is extremely variable; to compress, once again, their wage costs and enable their apprentices to be "paid off" as quickly as possible, the entrepreneurs tend to specialize them very early on in piecemeal tasks. This results in devaluation of the training provided and veritable exploitation of the young. Accordingly, any endeavour to increase work productivity implies that apprenticeship be controlled and supported by supplementary training activities.

Several proposals for educational measures in support of the traditional sector have been formulated over the past few years. Many of them are not invalidated by the results of the studies. Valid measures appear to be, in particular, adult literacy programmes, radio or newspaper information campaigns on existing legislation, methods of organizing co-operatives, possibilities of obtaining technical assistance or credits, training streams available, etc., proposals for the setting-up of vocational-training centres with a flexible structure, offering part-time education or evening classes to apprentices to supplement their general, theoretical and technical training, or to entrepreneurs who wish to improve their knowledge in specific fields. These courses might be organized in relatively short, complementary units, so as to be adapted to the participants' requirements. These proposals have the merit of endeavouring to raise the level of the basic education of workers in the traditional sector, and improve and control the quality of apprenticeship, while at the same time retaining the flexibility and utility of this type of training, and providing entrepreneurs with opportunities for broadening their knowledge in various economic or technical fields depending on their own requirements and the level of their firm's development.

Several qualifications must be made, on the other hand, with respect to the method of introducing these proposals. The problems of organizing literacy programmes are well known. Without going over all the problems, we may mention the difficulties in guaranteeing satisfactory attendance by the workers concerned when their participation will have no immediate effect on their level of pay, the reluctance of employers to free their employees during the working day, etc. This requires special solutions in terms of financing methods, and place and time of classes. As for the attempts to control apprenticeship, they will face much stronger opposition by the entrepreneurs, who will look upon this as an instrument to control their use of labour, a means of increasing competition, and a major factor in increasing wage costs: a direct increase due to lost earnings, even if the remuneration of the apprentices enrolled in these courses will be reduced (this remuneration is already, at present, very low or nil), or a longer-term increase if the trained apprentice, after a far shorter period than at present, demands a wage rise or leaves his master. Many entrepreneurs are in this case likely to refuse to take on apprentices without laying down certain conditions or preventing them from enrolling for this type of training. Several measures might be considered to encourage entrepreneurs to take part in this type of programme. Credit grants or the awarding of public contracts might be made subject to their taking part in these programmes; or access to the traditional sector might even be controlled and made subject to the possession of such or such a training. The risk of this policy, however, is obvious: that of favouring the most succesful entrepreneurs, permitting the establishment of agents from outside the traditional sector (small capitalists, civil servants), who will meet the requisite conditions and will be able to bear the slightly higher costs, and dooming the less productive units to extinction. Many firms manage to survive only because of their extremely low costs and the exploitation of very cheap labour; by increasing, however slightly, their costs and enabling certain producers to emerge, one implicitly accepts the extinction of these firms and a rise in under-employment. At the other extreme, to permit the development of an apprenticeship which is merely a disguised form of wage earning with a very small training component, amounts to accepting the exploitation of young apprentices, the proliferation of apprentice-entrepreneurs who set up their own business in the hope of improving their conditions, and the long-term deterioration in productivity, product quality and the working and living conditions of a large proportion of the population. This may lead either to the breaking-up of the traditional sector by integration into the modern sector, or to the maintenance of a sector at the subsistence level.

Between these two extremes, there are various half-way solutions. Everything in fact depends on the economic policy adopted by the country, and the traditional sector's prospects for evolution. Should one promote a few more dynamic firms and help them enter the modern sector, even by making a large proportion of the other firms marginal, thereby increasing unemployment? Or should one on the contrary assist the greatest number of firms in increasing their production and employment, even if this means very low productivity levels and incomes? Or, lastly, should one emphasize the modern sector, assuming that in the long run the employment problem in the traditional sector will gradually be solved from the inside? This choice is a political choice, depending very largely on the country's growth strategy, and which will have very different implications for educational planning.

What types of action can be recommended to the educational planner? Undoubtedly, this document, aiming rather at evaluating the studies and research undertaken on the traditional sector, does not intend to make proposals with a view to solving all the problems. However, there appear to be two types of suggestions springing from the studies examined in this document: suggestions for both short- and long-term measures.

The objective of the short-term measures would be to facilitate the transition from school to work, and the school-leavers' integration into the world of work. Depending on the socio-political systems in which these measures are undertaken, emphasis will be placed on literacy campaigns, post-primary or post-secondary short technical courses, regulations concerning the apprenticeship system in conjunction with various measures of incitement or even control of access to certain jobs, or a highly flexible vocational-training system based on evening classes, aiming at the apprentices and workers in the traditional sector, information campaigns and various short courses aiming more particularly at the entrepreneurs in the sector.

The longer-term measures would aim at developing and improving universal basic education. Many of the workers in the traditional sector will not be directly concerned by the programmes mentioned above. The workers in question are those who have a job which is not directly productive in the sector which we have called residual: shoeshiners, pedlars, domestic staff. The ultimate objective is to reduce employment in this sector. However, in view of the very limited prospects for taking on labour in the modern or even intermediate sector, it is probable that this type of employment will continue to develop in the future, or at least remain at the same level. If it is implicitly recognized that a considerable section of the population will continue to be unemployed or under-employed, educational policy should endeavour to ensure a certain equalization of opportunities, and provide possibilities for mobility and social advancement. Many other workers in the traditional sector are destined to be either directly integrated or subjected to the modern sector and proletarianized. Here again, the objective of planning policy should be to ensure greater social mobility, better opportunities for transition between the modern and traditional sectors, or for promotion within the traditional sector. An essential condition of this mobility is that everyone be provided with the same basic training, which should be as long as possible: teaching to read, write and count, providing a certain economic and social training which will be valuable to them in becoming organized, acquiring information, and finding another job, and developing the spirit of enterprise by more open training methods, participative teaching, etc.

It is our firm belief that it is neither possible nor legitimate to train given groups of the population for the traditional sector, any more than it is legitimate in a highly stratified and unequal society to select *a priori* and train "target-groups" to work in the rural sector or the modern sector, or in executive positions. In the first place, as we have seen, the traditional sector only acquires its meaning from the modern sector, and far from there being two very distinct sectors, there is a continuum of situations ranging from subsistence jobs to the highest-paid jobs in the modern sector, and opportunities of moving back and forth from one situation to another should remain open, if not be encouraged. Secondly, the traditional sector's prospects for development are far too uncertain for one to consider freezing workers in positions with no prospects for reconversion, mobility and promotion. Finally, the best method of training for the traditional sector is, with a few changes, in the traditional sector itself, just as the best training in order to become a worker in the modern sector is within the modern sector itself. If there is a grain of truth in the above remarks, the objective of an educational policy should accordingly be to break any *strict* relationship between development of education and employment. The role of preparing for a job will lie with vocational training of very short duration. In the first instance, education should aim at cultural development and the individual growth of each person. Secondly, it should aim at changing, not reproducing, the existing economic and social structures. In view of the fact that the traditional sector will continue to exist for a long time in numerous countries, and be characterized by highly unfavourable work and income conditions, the question is not so much "How to train for the traditional sector?" as "Who is in the traditional sector?", and care should be taken to see that it is not always the same population groups which are under-employed or unemployed.

In this document we have endeavoured to contribute towards

answers to the questions "Who is in the traditional sector; what path did they follow to get there; how did they acquire their vocational knowledge; and, what is the role of education/training in access to and development of the traditional sector?" Existing research, however, is still very inadequate to completely cover these questions. Without more thorough knowledge concerning these points it is extremely dangerous to make concrete proposals, especially concerning strategies for short-term training for the traditional sector. In this respect various lines of research appear promising:

1. Study of educational and job itineraries followed by workers in the traditional sector. The object of these studies would be to identify how the various types of workers in the traditional sector have acquired their knowledge: pure self-worker with varying degrees of success, entrepreneur maintaining more or less close relationships with the modern sector (including subcontracting), or mere worker in this sector. Our main assumption is that the entrepreneur's educational background and professional experience will affect the way in which his firm develops and is run. If there are dominant itineraries, who takes these itineraries in priority, and what are the consequences for the firm's level of activity and characteristics? What conclusions can be drawn for educational policy?

    This research should be carried out by means of a small-scale survey of traditional firms, nevertheless permitting adequate coverage of the sector. The survey should be supplemented by more monographic studies, worker interviews centring on their occupational history, monographs of firms emphasizing the method of organization and operation of the production unit, and the very process of training and apprenticeship.

2. Analysis of types of qualifications required for various jobs in the traditional sector. We have seen that there are a large variety of jobs, each with different educational requirements. Knowledge of this hierarchy of qualifications is essential for working out vocational-training programmes. Studies should emphasize not only the technical knowledge required, but also all the non-cognitive characteristics.

3. Evaluation of educational programmes in support of the traditional sector. In Latin America various vocational-training organizations (SENA, INACAP) have got under way pro-

grammes specially concerned with the requirements of the traditional sector. In East Africa and Asia several institutions provide training specifically designed for those who wish to become self-employed workers. It would be worth assessing the impact of this type of programme, by a follow-up study of those taking part.
4. Many studies are beginning to appear concerning the urban traditional sector, but little is known concerning the functioning of commerce, the services and the handicraft sector in rural areas. It would be worth carrying out research on this sector so as to show how it functions, how it develops, what are its upstream links with the agricultural sector and downstream links with the urban traditional sector and modern sector, and how job qualifications are acquired.

Education, training and the traditional sector

APPENDIX 1. Nomenclature of small-scale activities.

Branches and occupations	Status of work	Capital intensiveness	Infra-urban	Wages	Bourgeoisie	State	Export
1. SERVICES							
11. Personal services							
111. Domestic services (porter, domestics)	Wage-earners	Nil	—	(×)	×	(×)	×
112. Care services (hairdresser, healer, shoeshine boy)	Independent + apprentice	Low	×	×	(×)	×	—
113. Artistic services (photographer, artist, public entertainers...)	Independent	Low or nil	×	×	—	—	—
114. Cultural services (public letter-writer)	Independent	Nil	×	—	—	—	—
115. Leisure services (prostitute, guide)	Dependent	Nil	(×)	(×)	×	(×)	×
116. Illegal services (detective, black market dealer, pimp, money dealer)	Independent	Nil	—	—	×	×	×
12. Maintenance and repair services							
121. Shoes, leather goods (rubber, cobbler, tyres)	Independent + apprentice	Low	(×)	×	×	×	×
122. Electrical goods	Independent + apprentice	Low	—	(×)	×	×	×
123. Vehicules, cars and motor cycles, and bicycles (e.g. garage-owners and mechanics)	Independent + apprentice	Medium or low	—	(×)	×	×	×
124. Clocks and watches (e.g. watchmaker)	Independent + apprentice	Low	—	(×)	×	×	×
125. Clothing, linen (e.g. laundry)	Independent + apprentice	Low or medium	—	(×)	×	×	×
126. Building (electrician, plumber, tiler)	Sub-contractor	Low	—	×	×	×	×

Appendix

		Quasi wage-earners + assistants Semi-permanent or occasional labour	Dependence on customer	More or less dependent on the commercial circuits of the modern sector		
21.	Dealers in scrap from the modern sector	—	—	—	—	—
211.	Producers of farm produce and foodstuffs	Very low or nil	x	(x)	—	—	—
212.	Clothing		x	(x)	—	—	—
213.	Timber		x	(x)	—	—	—
214.	Paper, cardboard		x	(x)	—	—	—
215.	Chemicals		x	(x)	—	—	—
216.	Other products		x	(x)	—	—	—
22.	Processors of products for customers	Low or medium					
221.	Farm, food		x	x	x	x	x
222.	Garments		(x)	x	x	x	x
223.	Timber		(x)	x	x	x	x
3. TRADE							
31.	Depending on status						
311.	Pedlars	Very low	x	x	—	—	—
312.	Hawkers	Very low	x	x	—	—	—
313.	Coxeur	Very low	x	—	—	—	—
314.	Stallholder	Medium					
315.	Small shopkeeper						
32.	Depending on products						
321.	Foodstuffs		x	x	—	—	—
322.	Textiles						
323.	Timber						
324.	Paper, cardboard		x	x	—	—	—
325.	Chemicals		x	x	(x)	(x)	(x)
326.	Metals		x	—	—	—	—

APPENDIX 1. *(continued)*

Branches and occupations	Status of work	Capital intensiveness	Infra-urban	Wages Bourgeoisie	State	Export
4. TRANSPORT						
41. Land transport	Independent + assistance					
411. Passengers (rickshaw, horse-drawn cart, driver)	Independent	Low	x	(×)	(×)	(×)
412. Goods (bullock or donkey cart, porters, pedlars)	Independent	Low or nil	x	—	—	—
42. Inland waterways (pirogue paddler, boatman)	Independent	Low	x	x	—	—
43. Warehouse	Independent	Low	x	(×)	—	—
5. PRODUCERS OF COMMODITIES						
51. Agricultural, food processing industries (bakers, makers of fritters, coffee sorters, dehuskers)	(artisan) more or less dependent on commercial capital and different utilization of apprentices and assistance	Medium	(×)	x	(×)	—
52. Textiles, clothing, leathergoods		Medium				
521. Textiles: weaver		Medium	(×)(×)	x x	(×)(×)	— —
522. Clothing: tailor (men's or women's)			(×)(×)	x x	(×)(×)	— —
523. Leather: cobbler, bootmaker		Medium	(×)	x	(×)	—
53. Timber (cabinet-maker, joiner, sculptor, carpenter)		Medium	(×)	x	x	x
54. Paper, printing						
541. Publishing			—	—	x	x
542. Paper and papyrus maker, binder				x	x	x

551. Soap, cosmetics makers	—					
552. Makers of traditional drugs						
56. Non-metallic minerals						
561. Potters, basketweavers	×	×	×	×	×	
562. Building materials: brickmakers						
57. Metalworking						
571. Toymakers	×	×	—	—	—	
572. Metal furniture-makers	×	×	—	—	—	
573. Makers of metal construction materials	×	×	—	—	—	Medium — Artisan
574. Makers of transport equipment						Medium — Artisan
58. Arts and crafts						
581. Jeweller	—	(×)	×	×	×	Medium
582. Musical instrument makers, makers of objets d'art	×	×	×	×	×	Medium — Artisan
6. BUILDING AND PUBLIC WORKS	×	×	×	×	×	Medium — Journeymen Artisans

Masons, brickmakers, painters, floor and roof tilers, welldiggers.

APPENDIX 2. *Typology of urban adult male population*

NOTE : The areas of the circles are proportionate to the size of each category.
Average monthly resources of heads of households are given in 1971 CFA Francs and US **$**.

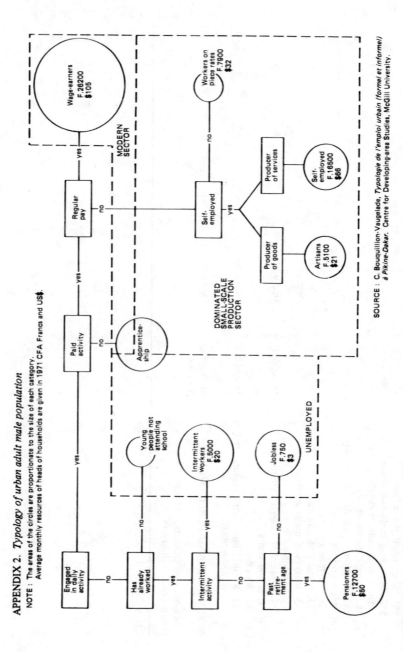

SOURCE : C. Bouquillion-Vaugelade, *Typologie de l'emploi urbain (formel et informel) à Pikine-Dakar*, Centre for Developing-area Studies, McGill University.

Appendix

TABLE A.1. Age structure of urban working population (percentages)

Age in years	Family workers	Apprentices	Employers	Self-employed	Working population
Iran, 1976					
Under 25	72.7	n.a.	6.1	13.0	28.0
25-44	20.5	n.a.	54.6	46.5	47.4
45 and over	6.7	n.a.	39.3	40.5	24.0
Syria, 1970					
Under 25	75.8	92.2	3.7	12.2	29.3
25-44	22.1	7.8	57.2	48.2	48.7
45 and over	2.1	—	39.1	39.6	22.0
Brazzaville, 1974					
Under 25	82.7 [1]	—	3.7	11.7	13.1
25-44	17.3 [1]	—	63.4	57.9	64.6
45 and over	—	—	32.9	30.4	22.3
Caracas, 1970					
Under 25	48.5	n.a.	12.9	15.0	31.0
25-44	33.2	n.a.	65.6	51.7	49.4
45 and over	18.3	n.a.	21.5	33.3	19.6

1. Family workers and apprentices.
SOURCE Census returns: Iran 1976, Syria 1970, Congo 1974, Venezuela 1970 (national publications).

TABLE A.2. Jakarta, Indonesia: breakdown of work-force by status and age, 1971.

Age	Self-employed	Employers	Family workers	Salaried workers	Un-employed	Total
10-14	5.5	0.3	15.4	42.2	36.6	100.0
15-19	10.3	0.9	9.5	58.4	20.9	100.0
20-24	13.9	1.5	6.2	61.2	17.2	100.0
25-29	16.9	2.2	3.6	67.1	10.2	100.0
35-39	23.0	3.3	3.0	61.6	9.1	100.0
45-49	25.2	4.8	2.9	59.8	7.3	100.0
50-54	28.2	4.8	3.1	53.8	10.1	100.0

SOURCE S.V. Sethuraman: Jakarta, Urban development and Employment, ILO (2).

Education, training and the traditional sector

TABLE A.3. Women as a percentage of non-agricultural working population.

Country and year	Employers and self-employed	Family workers	Employees and salaried workers
Algeria (66)	4.5	10.3	8.6
Tunisia (75)	40.1	73.4	14.9
Egypt (66)	5.8	37.0	11.2
Syria (Damascus) (70)	3.2	6.9	10.2
Tanzania (67)	18.7	44.1	10.7
Congo (Brazzaville) (74)	43.9	n.a.	10.3
Argentina (70)	19.4	40.8	30.4
Bolivia (76)	39.7	n.a.	27.5
Brazil (70)	22.7	25.1	31.7
Costa Rica (73)	13.0	29.4	32.7
Chile (70)	27.5	38.6	28.9
Ecuador (74)	24.9	39.1	29.5
Mexico (75)	32.2	44.7	31.4
Venezuela (75)	28.9	62.6	33.4
India (71)	9.8	22.2	9.6
Indonesia (71)	39.2	61.9	25.0
Korea (76)	39.1	78.0	28.4
Nepal (71)	12.8	25.3	7.4
Philippines (76)	56.7	69.3	42.6
Thailand (76)	43.4	76.6	30.2

SOURCE ILO Yearbook, 1977.

TABLE A.4. Percentage of women in non-agricultural active population.

	Family workers	Employers	Self-employed	Salaried workers	Total
Brazzaville (1974)	n.a.	7.1	44.6	10.3	23.0
Venezuela (1971) [1]	64.5	10.8	14.7	30.8	27.4
Damascus, Syria (1970)	14.2	1.4	3.6	10.2	8.7
Tunisia (1975) [1]	73.4	3.6	44.6	14.9	20.8

1. Non-agricultural PEA.
SOURCE Published census returns.

TABLE A.5. Nouakchott: educational profile of traditional sector workers (percentages), 1977.

	Apprentices	Unskilled workers	Skilled workers	Clerical	Heads of businesses
No education	79.6	69.7	36.2	48.5	22.1
Elementary education	19.4	16.9	47.7	21.2	65.6
Secondary education	0.0	—	4.6	21.2	12.3
Answer too vague	1.0	13.4	11.5	9.1	—
Total	100.0	100.0	100.0	100.0	100.0
Number of cases	201	142	218	33	

SOURCE Nihan (*11*).

TABLE A.6. Kumasi, Ghana: type of vocational training received according to businessmen's educational background (percentages), 1975.

Basic educational background	Type of vocational training		
	Training in an institution	Appenticeship in modern sector	Apprenticeship in traditional sector
No education	—	26.7	29.7
Primary education	10.0	6.7	12.6
Middle school	50.0	66.7	57.6
Technical	40.0	—	0.7
Total	100.0	100.0	100.0
Number of cases	10	15	169

SOURCE Arye (*22*)

TABLE A.7. Working conditions in the traditional sector, Tanzania (percentages), 1970.

	Hours worked per day			Days worked per week		Number of years self-employed	
	5 or less	6-10	11 or more	3 or less	6-7	More than 3	Less than 1
Crafts/manufacture	22.0	72.0	7.0	12.0	82.0	67.0	13.0
Shopkeeping	10.0	56.0	34.0	8.0	89.0	71.0	13.0
Pedlars	28.0	50.0	22.0	5.0	85.0	53.0	24.0
Construction	17.0	81.0	3.0	22.0	67.0	71.0	9.0
Hôtel/Bar	20.0	52.0	28.0	8.0	88.0	57.0	29.0
Total wage-earners	7.0	86.0	7.0	3.0	85.0	47.0	27.0

SOURCE Bienefeld (23).

TABLE A.8. Working conditions in the traditonal sector, Ouagadougou and Dakar.

	Average number of years self-employed	No. of hours worked per week by employers
Ouagadougou (1975)		
Arts and crafts	14.9	
Weavers	5.9	
Tailors	5.9	
Trade	6.5	
Construction	3.4	
Small-scale services	5.1	
Dakar (1977)		
Metalworkers	12.6	53.5
Carpenters	10.4	50.2
Furniture-makers	6.8	53.7
Brickmakers	9.2	44.3
Masons	10.0	48.5
Mechanical repairs	8.0	56.5
Electrical repairs	6.8	52.1
Watch repairs	9.6	57.2

SOURCE Van Dijk (24), (25).

Bibliography

(*1*) PREALC, Oficina Internacional de Trabajo, *Sector informal: funcionamiento y politicas,* 1978.
Brings together the results of the PREALC's studies on Asunción (Paraguay), San Salvador, Quito, Guayaquil (Ecuador), Santo Domingo (Dominican Republic), Mexico, Guadalajara, Monterrey. Study based on surveys of census households. The criterion employed in defining the informal sector is either an income criterion or a criterion of job category. Domestic staff are included in the informal sector.

(*2*) ILO, S. V. Sethuraman, *Jakarta: urban development and employment,* 1976.
This study forms part of the ILO's research programme on "urbanization and employment", which covers several cities throughout the world. The work examines the development of the City of Jakarta, analyzing the various sectors of activity, the infrastructure, the population and the work force. A special chapter is devoted to the traditional sector.

(*3*) D. Mazumdar, *Analysis of the dual labour market in LDCs,* (mimeograph).
This is a theoretical paper presented at the 4th World Congress of the IIRS in 1976. The author discusses the consequences of several hypotheses on the functioning of the labour market.

(*4*) ILO, *Employment, income and equality: a strategy for increasing productive employment in Kenya,* 1972.
This is a report by a multi-sectorial mission of the ILO, organized within the framework of the World Employment Programme. The work also|includes|several appendixes which deal in detail with various aspects of a full-employment strategy in Kenya. Owing to the position which the authors recommend for the traditional (informal) sector, this report had a major impact when it was published.

(5) P. Hugon, *Eléments du débat méthodologique à propos du secteur informel et de la petite production marchande dans les pays sous-dévéloppés,* IEDES, mimeograph, March 1979.
This paper discusses various theoretical viewpoints concerning the traditional (informal) sector, ranging from the dualistic analyses to the radical schools.

(6) C. Gerry, *Disguised wage employment: an exploratory note,* IEDES, mimeograph, March 1979.
This paper centres on the role of "intermediaries" as factors in reducing the autonomy of the "self-employed", whom they transform into "virtual wage-earners". The author shows this by taking examples in the City of Dakar (shoemakers, the artisan sector), and works out an interesting typology of the components of the work force.

(7) IEDES, *La petite production marchande et l'emploi dans le secteur informel: le cas africain,* Volumes I and II, by P. Hugon *et al.,* 1978.
This is the result of a major research effort by an IEDES team on the various theoretical and empirical works on the traditional sector. This reference work includes numerous statistical illustrations, an effort at conceptualization, and a valuable bibliography.

(8) ILO, *Sharing in development: a programme of employment, equity and growth in the Philippines,* 1974.
This is a report by a multi-sectorial mission of the ILO organized within the framework of the World Employment Programme. The work includes several appendixes, and contains original data on the economy and employment in the Philippines.

(9) W. Steel, *Intensité de capital, dimension de la firme et choix entre l'emploi et la production: l'importance d'un cadre multi-sectoriel pour la politique et la recherche économiques,* IEDES, mimeograph, March 1979.
This theoretical paper examines on the basis "of a model" the consequences of various economic policies centring on the traditional sector, in particular to fight unemployment.

(*10*) H. Chenery *et al. Redistribution with growth,* Oxford University Press, 1974.
The authors, for the most part World Bank economists, outline and discuss various aspects of growth strategies aiming at ensuring a certain amount of equality in distribution of the benefits of growth.

(*11*) G. Nihan in conjunction with D. Dviry and R. Jourdain, *Le secteur non structuré moderne de Nouakchott, République islamique de Mauritanie. Rapport d'enquête et analyse des résultats,* ILO, 1978.
1977 survey of 131 entrepreneurs in sectors with potential for pro-

viding employment in industrial production and the artisan sector, the repair services and various branches of the building industry. Criteria adopted: permanent or semi-permanent location; internal structure and management technique.

(*12*) J. Hallak, *A qui profite l'école?*, PUF, 1974.
Work on educational economics, centring on two main themes: equity and development.

(*13*) O. Lebrun and C. Gerry, "Petty producers and capitalism", *Review of African political economy*, no. 3, May-October 1975.
This article sums up the basic points in the authors' thesis on the evolution of the artisan sector in Africa.

(*14*) S. Amin, *L'échange inégal et la loi de la valeur*, Anthropes, 1973.
This work contains, among other things, a radical reading of international exchanges, within the theroretical framework of "centre-periphery relations".

(*15*) A. Morice, see (7).

(*16*) K. King, *The African artisan*, Heinemann, 1977.
By means of an approach similar to that of anthropological surveys, the author studies the life histories of some artisans (in Kenya) and puts forward an interesting reading of the relationships between the traditional sector and the modern sector.

(*17*) O. Lebrun, *Mécanismes de dissolution conservation — développement de l'artisanat et problématique de l'éducation — formation dans les zones urbaines d'Afrique*, Unesco-IDEP, Douala, 1973, mimeograph.
Presentation of one of the most interesting theses concerning the evolution of the traditional sector in Africa.

(*18*) J. Charmes, *Les contradictions du développement du secteur non structuré*, IEDES, mimeograph, 1979.
This paper sums up the results of surveys of carpenters/cabinet makers and garage owners/mechanics, and illustrates Lebrun and Gerry's thesis on the evolution of the artisan sector in Africa.

(*19*) McGhee, *Peasants in the cities, a most ingenious paradox of human organisation*, Washington, 1973.

(*20*) IPEA, *Brazilian economic studies*, no. 4.

(*21*) Source: estimates by H. Joshi.

(*22*) G. Arye, *Effects of formal education and training on the intensity of employment in the informal sector: a case study of Kumasi, Ghana*. Geneva, ILO, 1976.
Survey of 300 entrepreneurs at Kumasi, Ghana. The sample covers the artisan and industrial production sectors, the repair services, and those firms (individual or other) with a fixed location.

(*23*) M. A. Bienefeld, *The self-employed of urban Tanzania*.
I.D.S. Discussion paper no. 54, University of Sussex, 1974.

1971 survey of unsalaried workers in urban areas. 700 people surveyed, in various activities of the informal sector, not including domestic services: artisan sector, construction, pedlars, regular commerce, hotels, building hire, agriculture.

(24) Van Dijk, *Enquête sur le secteur non structuré*, (Dakar), ILO Jobs and Skills Programme for Africa, mimeograph.

Survey of two districts of Dakar (Medina and Pikine) and eight main activities in the artisan sector, construction, repair services, clockmakers, masons, woodworkers, moulders, electrical repairmen, mechanical repairmen, upholsterers, and metal-workers. The only entrepreneurs interviewed were those with no legal status and whose workers regularly receive less than the minimum legal wage and do not benefit from Social Security (1977 survey).

(25) Van Dijk, *Enquête du secteur non structuré à Ouagadougou,* Vol. I, Analysis and diagnosis of the non-structured sector at Ouagadougou, Dakar, ILO/ONPE, February 1977.

Survey of 300 entrepreneurs in the artisan sector, construction industry, commerce, and repair services (1976).

(26) M. Penouil, "Quatre études sectorielles à Abidjan et Yaoundé", paper presented at the IEDES Symposium on small-scale commodity production in urban environments in Africa.

Report on surveys carried out by research workers from the Bordeaux University (including numerical data as to the occupational category, production conditions, and incomes), followed by some reflections on informal activities and their prospects.

(27) T.C. MacGee and Y.M. Yeung, *Hawkers in Southeast Asian cities planning for the bazaar economy.* IDRC, 1977.

This work is a comparative synthesis of some studies carried out under the auspices of the Canadian IDRC on the hawkers in certain large cities of Southeast Asia (Kuala Lumpur, Malacca, Manilla, Baguio, Jakarta and Bandong.

(28) K.Schaefer, in conjunction with Cheywa R. Spindel, *Sao Paulo: desarrollo urbano y empleo,* ILO, 1976.

Defines the informal sector according to two criteria:
— Criterion of activity: all self-employed workers, minus the professions, plus those establishments with less than nine employees.
— Criterion of income: activities with a mean income below a certain threshold.

(29) G. Salem, "Contribution à l'étude des réseaux commerciaux dans la ville africaine: exemples de Dakar", paper presented at the IEDES Symposium, 1979.

This paper sums up the results of a socio-anthropological study of the organization of Senegalese commercial networks in France.

(30) R. Devauges, "Le neveu et l'apprenti: un statut en évolution dans

la petite entreprise congolaise", paper presented at the IEDES Symposium, 1979.
This paper, based on a continuous survey of 40 artisans, from 1968 to 1971, and 16 apprentices at Brazzaville, studies the conditions of recruitment and work of apprentices in the Congo.

(*31*) J. Hallak, *Migration from rural areas: employment and education,* IIEP Seminar Paper, 1976.
Brief outline of the main theses on migrations, enriched by illustrations.

(*32*) J. Gaude, *Causes and repercussions of rural migration in developing countries: a critical analysis,* WEP, October 1975, ILO.
This report sums up and compares the results of several surveys on factors of migration from rural areas.

(*33*) P. Brigg, *Some economic interpretations of case studies of urban migration in developing countries,* IBRD Staff Working Paper, no. 151, March 1973.
Interesting effort to work out a typology of the factors of migration from rural to urban areas.

(*34*) K. Davis, *World urbanisation 1950-1970, Volume I, Basic data for cities, countries and regions,* Population Monograph Series no. 4, Berkeley UCLA/11S 1969.

(*35*) N. Carynnyk-Sinclair, *Rural to urban migration in developing countries 1950-1970: a survey of the literature,* WEP, ILO 1974.
"State of work". Contains a relatively full comparison of the results of several studies.

(*36*) H. Sidibe, *Etude du potentiel d'emploi du secteur non structuré moderne en vue de la planification des ressources humaines: cas de Bamako,* mimeograph, IEDES, 1979.

(*37*) A. Tabi-Abodo, *L'auto-emploi et le secteur non structuré des zones urbaines du Caméroun,* IEDES mimeograph, 1979.
After summing up the various works on the traditional sector in Cameroon, the author presents certain results, in particular of the AFCA-CAPME survey in 1976. In appendix, a draft questionnaire for a survey in conjunction with the ILO.

(*38*) C. de Miras, "Essai de définition du secteur de subsistance dans les branches de production à Abidjan", paper presented at the IEDES Symposium, 1979
This paper, based on the results of research carried out at Abidjan since 1975 in several production branches (joinery, automotive repairs and bakeries) sets out thoughts on production conditions in the subsistence sector and the processes of evolution of this same sector.

(*39*) A. Callaway, "Nigeria's indigenous education: the apprenticeship

system" *University of Ibadan Journal of African Studies,* Vol. 1, 1964.
Presentation of the results of a complete study of the artisan sector and the small industrial establishments at Ibadan in 1961.

(*40*) J. R. Harris, "Industrial entrepreneurship in Nigeria", Ph. D. thesis.
Results of a survey covering 268 Nigerian industrial firms in 1965, most of which employed over 20 workers.

(*41*) P. Lachaud, *Contribution à l'étude du secteur informel en Côte-d'Ivoire: le cas du secteur de l'habillement à Abidjan,* Bordeaux University I, Sciences économiques, 1976.

(*42*) S. Kannappan (edited by), *Studies of urban labour market behaviour in developing areas,* International Institute for Labour Studies, 1977.
This book brings together 17 articles analyzing the relationships between the structures of the labour market, their consequences for unemployment, and the distribution of resources in urban areas in developing countries.

(*43*) O. J. Fapohunda, H. Lubell (with contributions by J. Reijmering and M. P. Van Dijk), *Lagos: urban development and employment,* ILO, Geneva, 1978.
This study analyzes the problems of urbanization and employment in Lagos, capital of Nigeria, studying, in particular, the informal sector in this city and certain other States.

(*44*) Garcia, Oliveira, Stern, "Migration et marginalité professionnelle dans la ville de Mexico", in *Espaces et sociétés,* July 1971.

(*45*) G. Nihan, in conjunction with E. Demol, D. Dviry and C. Jourdain, *Le secteur non structuré modern de Lomé, République Togolaise: rapport d'enquêtes et analyse des résultats.* ILO, 1978.
This paper sets out the results of a survey carried out in 1978 on 280 production, service and construction firms in the traditional sector. In all, 22 sectors were included, constituting the "modern" non-structured sector, that is, producing goods and services parallelling those of the organized sector, and having prospects for development. The report analyzes the firms' economic characteristics and also studies, in particular, the role of training in the non-structured sector.

IIEP publications and documents

More than 500 titles on all aspects of educational planning have been published by the International Institute for Educational Planning. A comprehensive catalogue, giving details of their availability, includes research reports, case studies, seminar documents, training materials, occasional papers and reference books in the following subject categories:

Economics of education, costs and financing
Manpower and employment
Demographic studies
The location of schools and sub-national planning
Administration and management
Curriculum development and evaluation
Educational technology
Primary, secondary and higher education
Vocational and technical education
Non-formal, out-of-school, adult and rural education

Copies of the catalogue may be obtained from the IIEP on request.

The International Institute for Educational Planning

The International Institute for Educational Planning (IIEP) is an international centre for advanced training and research in the field of educational planning. It was established by Unesco in 1963 and is financed by Unesco and by voluntary contributions from individual Member States.

The Institute's aim is to contribute to the development of education throughout the world by expanding both knowledge and the supply of competent professionals in the field of educational planning. In this endeavour the Institute co-operates with interested training and research organizations in Member States. The Governing Board of the IIEP, which approves the Institute's programme and budget, consists of eight elected members and four members designated by the United Nations Organization and certain of its specialized agencies and institutes.

Chairman Malcom Adiseshiah (India), Vice-Chancellor, University of Madras; Director, Institute of Development Studies, Madras

Designated members
Samir Amin, Director of Research, CODESRIA, Dakar
P. N. Dhar, Assistant Secretary-General for Research and Analysis, United Nations
T. Fülöp, Director, Division of Health Manpower Development, World Health Organization
Aklilu Habte, Director, Education Department, International Bank for Reconstruction and Development

Elected members
Candido Mendes de Almeida (Brazil), Director, President of Foundation Sociedade Brasileira de Instruçao, Rio de Janeiro
Jean-Claude Eicher (France), Director, Institute for Research in the Economics of Education, University of Dijon
M. A. El-Rashid (Saudi Arabia), Director, Arab Bureau of Education and Culture for Gulf States, Riyadh
Michael Kinunda (Tanzania), Chief Administrative Officer, University of Dar-es-Salaam
Sippanondha Ketudat (Thailand), Minister of Education, Bangkok
Jan Szczepanski (Poland), Vice-President, Polish Academy of Sciences
Victor Urquidi (Mexico), Presidente, El Colegio de Mexico, Mexico

Inquiries about the Institute should be addressed to:
The Director, IIEP, 7-9, rue Eugène-Delacroix, 75916 Paris